# THE COMPLETE POTTER:
# GLAZES

# THE COMPLETE POTTER:
# GLAZES

EMMANUEL COOPER

B. T. Batsford Ltd, London

Typeset by Servis Filmsetting Ltd,
Manchester
and printed in Hong Kong

Published by B. T. Batsford Ltd
4 Fitzhardinge Street, London W1H OAH

British Library Cataloguing-in-Publication
Data.

A catalogue record for this book is available
from the British Library.

ISBN 0 7134 6717 7

*(Front cover)* **Emmanuel Cooper** – City Sky,
*jug, thrown and modelled porcelain with
nickel glaze over zinc slip, 20 cm (8 in.) tall,
1990.*

*(Back cover)* **Janice Tchalenko** – *thrown
and turned stoneware bowl, 1989.*

*(Previous page)* **Derek Clarkson** – *bottle,
thrown and turned porcelain with crystalline
glaze, about 10 cm (4 in.) tall, 1991.* RECIPE:
*Ferro frit 3110 43.5, calcined zinc oxide 28.5,
flint 19.5, titanium dioxide 7.5, alumina
hydrate 0.4, China clay 0.6, + cobalt
carbonate 0.2, manganese oxide 1.3. The
glaze is fired in an electric kiln to 1260°C
(2300°F), cooled to 1090°C (1994°F) and
temperature held for 1 hour 15 minutes,
cooled and held at 1060°C (1940°F) for 1 hour
20 minutes, cooled to 1050°C (1922°F) and
held for 1 hour 30 minutes, cooled to 1040°C
(1900°F) and held for 20 minutes then
allowed to cool*

# CONTENTS

# INTRODUCTION

Of all the processes used by studio potters, glazing and firing are perceived as being the most difficult. Selecting, applying and firing glazes seem to present a series of insurmountable problems – each one part of a mystery in which luck rather than judgement seems to play a major role. Working with clay directly by modelling with the fingers, by throwing on the potter's wheel or by hand building, has an immediate sense of reality, offering a tangible involvement with the material. These are all basic attractions of the craft. In contrast, glazing may appear unrelated and separate. When dry or biscuit fired, the pot or object is at its least interesting; no longer workable as a material and without the sensuous qualities of plastic clay, the matt surface seems dull and lifeless, and some sort of finish is required to bring it to life as well as enabling

2 **Emmanuel Cooper** – *thrown and turned high-fired porcelain bowl, yellow glaze with black/bronze pigment rim, 12 cm (5 in.) across, 1990. A pleasing combination of a rich glossy colour and dark matt border*

the pot to be used. This is where glaze comes into its own and is able to transform surfaces, making them attractive to look at and practical for use.

Glaze has been in use in different parts of the world for over four thousand years and includes an enormous variety of colours and textures. Such an extensive range may seem bewildering to the less experienced potter and even those more familiar with the processes may be reluctant to leave established recipes to seek out other more experimental glazes. But this need not be the case. Glazing is one of the most fascinating and rewarding parts of the pottery process. Until pots are glazed they are only half finished, unless the absorbent surface is intentional such as in plant pots or sculptural heads. Glaze not only makes surfaces smooth, waterproof and hygienic, enabling them to be used for food and drink, but it also provides an opportunity to introduce colour, pattern, texture and decoration, as much a part of the creative aspects of the craft as modelling and throwing.

Potters acquire glazes from many sources;

they may be purchased as prepared powders which have only to be mixed with water, or even ready mixed for application to the pot. But many potters want to know more about the content of the glaze and discover how and why it works – for some this can be as fascinating as making the pot. But glazes are only as good as the way in which they are used and, while their origins may be illuminating, handling, application and firing are just as important. Any serious potter needs to have some knowledge of glazes – how they work, how different materials behave, how various effects and colours can be obtained, and the ways in which glaze can be modified to suit individual requirements. This not only gives potters greater control of the glazing process and so more confidence, but extends the range of possibilities. If the chemistry of glazes is related to practical experience then a deeper and more profound knowledge of glaze making is acquired.

This book sets out to dispel many of the myths around glaze and glazing by explaining in simple language what it is, and how it can be formulated and employed to full effect.

Materials used by studio potters are listed and their characteristics detailed. It also describes how potters can evolve their own glazes, how to prepare them from recipes, and the different ways of applying them to the pot. Colour in glaze is fully documented and many suggestions are given for successful results. The firing procedures are clearly explained enabling potters to make the best and most efficient use of their kiln. A final chapter lists different sorts of glaze, giving recipes and information on how they can be used and adapted to individual need.

As we have become more aware of the need for safety in handling ceramic materials and when firing pots, the need to take suitable precautions, particularly when handling glaze materials, cannot be stressed too highly. Many of the basic rules are common sense and these, coupled with good house keeping, are all that is required. Do not eat or drink in the pottery workshop, keep surfaces clean by wet wiping and avoid raising dust such as by gently tipping dry materials into water. Wash hands after handling all glaze materials, keep skin cuts well covered and do not ingest any material.

There are special problems when using lead; as frit it can be handled safely but must be used in properly formulated glazes. Raw lead should be avoided.

The particular dangers of other materials will be dealt with in the text. Respect the dangers of gas and oil when firing kilns and always turn off electricity at the main switch before packing or checking electric kilns.

During firing keep the kiln room well ventilated and ensure flammable materials are stored well away from the kiln.

The intention of *Glazes* is to combine sound practical advice with clear explanations of the technology involved. Theory is related to practice and experiments are suggested so potters can discover for themselves what happens when materials are put together. Successful glazing, whether following recipes, using ready-made commercial glazes or formulating your own mixtures is within reach of all potters. *Glazes* will, I hope, contribute to de-mystifying this most fascinating and exciting part of the potter's art.

*Emmanuel Cooper, London 1991*

# CHAPTER ONE

# KEEPING GLAZE SIMPLE

Calculating the chemical make up of a glaze as opposed to trial and error can be likened to the approach of a food scientist and a chef to cooking. Scientists can give an accurate indication of the chemical make up of a cake, for example, and calculate its nutritious value, but may not know how to bake it or what it will taste like. Chefs know exactly how to assemble the necessary ingredients, how to mix and bake the cake and are likely to have a good idea of its flavour, but they are unlikely to know its chemical contents. Maybe combining the two approaches would produce even better and tastier cakes. Potters with a list of ingredients necessary for a glaze, with little or no knowledge about what each contains and how and why they work, can profit from scientific knowledge.

Scientists describe glaze as *a complex, super-cooled, alumino-silicate glass*. Though scientifically accurate, it is of limited use to potters seeking to understand how glaze works, how it can be made up or in discovering glazes which are in accord with their technical and aesthetic requirements. Put more simply, a glaze is a sort of glass which

3 **Colin Pearson** – *thrown and turned high-fired porcelain bowl with pale blue glaze, about 12 cm (5 in) tall, 1990. The slightly runny glaze adds an element of surface movement to the strong but sensitive form*

is fired on the surface of clay to form a layer which may be shiny, opaque, matt, clear or coloured. It can consist of one or two but, more usually, is made up of three or more ingredients mixed with water to form a suspension. This liquid is applied to the pot usually after it has been biscuit fired, either by dipping, pouring, spraying or painting before being fired again. Two major exceptions are raw glaze and saltglaze. *Raw glaze* is applied to a green pot, that is one which has not been biscuited, and is then taken to top temperature in a single firing. *Saltglaze* is achieved through a vapour glaze and is not first covered with a liquid mixture; salt, usually sodium chloride (common salt), is introduced into the kiln at top temperature, around 1200°C (2190°F), when it volatilizes, reacting with the surface of the clay to form a thin glassy layer.

During the firing, as the temperature rises, the different ingredients which make up the glaze begin to affect each other and the mixture starts to form a glass. This combines with the surface of the clay, binding it in position. If taken to too high a temperature or if too thickly applied the glaze can become too fluid, start to run down the surface of the pot and attach itself to the kiln shelf. Glaze which is too thinly applied or fired to too low a temperature may appear dry and unattractive.

There are two approaches to understanding glaze. One is to treat it as a science, looking at its chemical and physical make up, the other is to follow a more pragmatic approach which involves discovering how materials behave when applied to clay and fired, so relating material and effect together. The scientific approach to glazes has a relatively short history and involves using chemical formulae to calculate how materials will react based on known information. Little more than 100 years ago chemists started to investigate how glazes work using new technological information to analyse materials and evolve chemical formulae for glaze. The German ceramic chemist Hermann Seger (1839–94) introduced the Seger formula, a method of describing the chemical make up of glaze still in use today.

The *Seger formula* divides the glaze into three component parts. Firstly the *fluxes* which belong to the class of chemicals known as bases and make the glaze melt; secondly the *amphoteric group* which is principally made up of alumina and binds the glaze on the surface of the pot, and thirdly *silica*, or acid, which forms the glass in the glaze. This system of calculating glaze was devised specifically for the ceramic industry with its

need for reliable, blemish-free glazes. With a knowledge of the chemical make up of glaze precise adjustment can be made as necessary.

Such a system of glaze construction depends on a reliable supply of materials, carefully controlled mixing and application of glaze and dependable kiln firings. It also makes use of the 'ideal' formula in which the components of the glaze are in balance, indicating why particular reactions take place and what may happen. It is also invaluable in enabling minor but crucial adjustments to be calculated. But it is of limited use to studio potters, few of whom want or require such a high degree of glaze control and are often unable or do not want to duplicate the precise conditions of industrial production. Glaze technology can teach us a great deal about how materials work, indicating the lines along which adjustments can be made. But studio potters by the nature of their work can often learn more from a practical approach, discovering by observation what happens to different materials and whether the results are those they seek.

For this reason a sound understanding of materials and how they behave in the kiln can be more valuable than pages of calculations. In saying this I do not want to suggest that a knowledge of glaze chemistry is of no value; calculating chemical formulae indicates how glazes are made up and may indicate adjustments which may be necessary. The chemical formulae of favourite glazes, for example, can be calculated as can those for

special effects to indicate why these have come about. Now that pocket calculators are cheap and familiar, once the steps have been understood and a suitable chart designed, the necessary arithmetic can be simply carried out. Methods for doing such calculations are clearly laid out in the appendix together with the relevant chemical information.

Because potters do not have to conform to standards of industrial production (other than safety requirements), they rarely need to calculate the chemical formula of glaze but may apply a knowledge of glaze chemistry to help understand how it is constructed. All materials have a chemical formula, providing a common language describing its chemical contents. Silica, the glass forming part of the glaze, has a formula Si and is present in an almost pure form in quartz and flint ($SiO_2$). Calcium (Ca), a powerful flux, is found in whiting which has the chemical formula $CaCO_3$. The chemical formula is instructive because it indicates that in whiting (sometimes called limestone) the calcium is combined with carbon dioxide, a gas liberated during the firing. Calcium is also present in dolomite which has the chemical formula $CaCO_3.MgCO_3$, revealing that not only is it combined with carbon dioxide but also with magnesium carbonate, $MgCO_3$, an equally powerful flux.

The chemical formula for China clay, $Al_2O_3.2SiO_2.2H_2O$, is more complex. It is made up of alumina, $Al_2O_3$, silica, $SiO_2$, and water, $H_2O$. It is useful to compare this with the chemical formula for potash feldspar, $K_2O.Al_2O_3.6SiO_2$. The two are similar in that they both contain alumina and silica, but dissimilar in that feldspar has no water content but, more importantly, contains potassium, $K_2O$, a powerful flux. Feldspar is made up of all three components necessary for making a glaze, that is a flux, present as potassium, the amphoteric in the form of alumina which keeps the glaze stable and prevents it running off the pot, and thirdly silica which is the glass former. The Chinese drew an analogy between the human body and the three parts of the glaze, calling the fluxes the blood, the amphoteric or alumina the flesh and the acid or silica the bones. Feldspar, which melts around 1250°C (2280°F) to form a stiff opaque glaze full of tiny trapped bubbles, is used in many high temperature glazes.

Reference to the chemical formula, once its language has been decoded, is enormously helpful in telling us what is present. All the elements, for example, are combined with oxygen, O, but in different proportions. Fluxes are either 1 to 1 or 2 to 1, ie CaO, MgO, ZnO, $K_2O$. Amphoteric are 2 to 3, ie alumina, $Al_2O_3$. Acids or glass formers are 1 to 2, ie silica, $SiO_2$. From this sort of knowledge it is possible to classify materials and make informed judgements about how they will behave in the glaze, though some appear not to conform to expectations. A list of the most useful chemical formulae of materials is given at the end of the book.

4 **Keiko Hasegawa** – *thrown lidded container, raku fired with a white tin-glaze, 1989. The characteristic effects of post-firing reduction work well on this pot; the tin glaze has developed an attractive crackle and the body has turned a rich black colour*

# TYPES OF POTTERY AND FIRING

Studio pottery, as opposed to industrial ceramics, is most usefully divided according to temperature rather than type of glaze. **Raku,** 900°C–1000°C (1652°F–1832°F), is low fired: the body is open and porous and the glazes highly decorative. Raku is fired by being placed in a glowing hot kiln, heated rapidly and, when the glaze has fluxed, removed and plunged into some sort of reducing material such as leaves or sawdust. **Earthenware,** 1020°C–1140°C (1870°F–2084°F), can be made up of either red terracotta clay or a white firing body. It is characterized by a slightly porous body with a distinct glaze layer on top of the body. **Medium stoneware,** 1180°C–1240°C (2156°F–2264°F), offers both the best of earthenware and the strength of higher fired wares, with a strong reaction between glaze and body. One of the advantages of this relatively little used temperature range is in fuel saving and hence lower costs of production. **Stoneware and porcelain,** 1240°C–1280°C (2264°F–2336°F). At this temperature the clay becomes hard and vitreous, porcelain may become translucent and the ware is stronger than low fired ceramics. A powerful reaction takes place between body and glaze, often with a layer formed between them, so that the clay affects the glaze, with any iron speckles in the body bleeding into it.

**Saltglaze** is a type of stoneware fired to the same temperature range. It is usually once fired in a special kiln and glazed by introducing common salt into the firing chamber near top temperature. The salt volatilizes and forms a thin layer of glaze which brings out the surface qualities of the clay. Stoneware glazes are usually applied on the insides of saltglaze pots.

Temperature alone offers only a limited indication of the fired result, but is crucial when devising glazes; though some will function over wide ranges of temperature, most are prepared for a specific fluxing point. Some fluxes, for example, are only effective above specific temperatures while others will start to volatilize if they become too hot and cease to be useful. Lead is a powerful flux but only at earthenware temperatures. Lithium, potassium, sodium and boron are active over the whole temperature range, while calcium, magnesium and zinc are most effective at higher temperatures.

In addition to the temperature, glaze materials and clay bodies are affected by the type of firing. Long slow firings allow materials to melt fully and at higher temperatures react with the clay body. Slow

5   **Tessa Fuchs** – Bridal Couple Tree, *earthenware with matt white glaze and painted underglaze decoration, about 30 cm (12 in.), 1989. The matt glaze and painted colour bring out the modelling and form of this fantasy piece*

cooling is equally important in enabling the glaze to become matt. Rapid firing and cooling, now easily obtainable in new super-efficient kilns, rarely produce subtle effects and can render glazes dull and lifeless.

Equally important is the atmosphere inside the kiln, chiefly influenced by the type of fuel used. Electricity, the most common energy source for studio potters, is convenient, easy to install and offers good value. Electric kilns are, simply, highly efficient insulated boxes with heating elements made from temperature resistant wire on the inside. The atmosphere, often erroneously called oxidizing, remains neutral. In contrast, flame-burning kilns, fired by gas, oil or wood, are more complex, with a through flow of heat from firebox to chimney and can be manipulated to create a reducing atmosphere. This limits the amount of oxygen available encouraging a greater degree of reaction between body and glaze, usually characterized by iron specking, and by the behaviour of certain metal colouring oxides. These varying effects are discussed more fully in Chapter 3.

## GLAZE MATERIALS IN COMMON USE

There are four main sorts of glaze materials in common use.

1 **Minerals** This group is made up of materials prepared from rocks of some kind. Such materials are carefully selected and ground to a fine powder or, in the case of some metal oxides, are refined from the appropriate ore. Some materials can be collected from suitable outcrops by geologist potters, but they are usually purchased from suppliers as fine powders. Most have a known chemical formula which can be used in glaze calculations. These can be sub-divided into materials which correspond to the fluxes, amphoterics and acids.

**Fluxes** (or bases) – potash feldspar, soda feldspar, Cornish stone (also called Cornwall stone or in the USA Carolina stone), petalite, nepheline syenite, whiting, dolomite, barium carbonate, talc, zinc oxide, lithium carbonate.

**Amphoteric** – China clay, white ball clay, red clay, bentonite, alumina hydrate.

**Acids** – flint, quartz.

2 **Frits** are commercially prepared glaze materials made to a known chemical formula; used in the glaze as fluxes, they make materials available to potters which are dangerous to handle or for some reason are not practical to use. Some, such as borax, potassium or sodium, are soluble in water or, like lead, are poisonous, while materials such as whiting contain volatile materials which, if pre-released, help to ensure a smooth glaze surface. Frits are made by mixing the soluble and/or poisonous fluxes with other materials, usually silica, and heating them in a large crucible until a molten glass is formed. This is then poured into cold water to shatter and break up the glass which is then ground to a fine powder. The common frits are lead bisilicate, borax frit, alkaline frit and calcium borate frit.

3 **Local materials**, which potters find for themselves, have no reliable chemical formulae and vary from batch to batch. Their interest lies precisely in their individual make up, particularly for potters who fire to stoneware temperatures, where they come closest to the sorts of materials used by oriental potters. This group includes plant ash, wood ash, local clay, granite powder and pumice.

4 **Metal oxides** are used for colouring or staining the glaze. These roughly fall in two groups; the *refractory opacifiers*, which suspend themselves in the glaze and refract light, notably tin oxide, zirconium oxide, titanium dioxide, chrome oxide, vanadium pentoxide and nickel oxide, and the *oxides*, which go into solution in the glaze and so allow light to pass through. These include cobalt oxide (and carbonate), copper oxide (and carbonate), manganese dioxide (and carbonate), iron oxide, ilmenite, yellow ochre, crocus martis, rutile.

## FINDING OUT FOR YOURSELF

The first step in understanding glaze materials is to discover as much about them as possible. The Chinese developed their glazes over many years, observing how materials behaved in the firing, a method which can be usefully linked to chemical formulae. By observing how materials behave when fired, practical knowledge can be built up and if this is related to even a basic grounding in glaze chemistry, the process of formulating and understanding glazes can be brought to life with surprising clarity.

An effective way of learning about materials is to fire each one on a clay tile; each material is mixed with water to a cream-like consistency and painted on the marked-out clay surface. A single layer is applied, then a second over half to give a double thickness. This will indicate any difference on the fired result according to the quantity of material present. Indicate on the tile the temperature and atmosphere of the kiln and label each material with a mixture of manganese and water. Manganese fuses permanently on the tile even at low temperature. The fired tile will demonstrate how each substance behaves when heated and how they react with the surface of the clay.

Arrange the materials on the tile more or less in the main groups listed earlier. By arranging similar materials together their behaviour can be more easily compared. Tiles should be made in the clay usually used and then biscuit fired. Make one for earthenware, say 1060°C (1940°F), one for medium stoneware, say 1200°C (2192°F), and two for stoneware (and/or porcelain), say 1260°C (2300°F), one for an electric kiln, another for a reduction firing. Mixing each material with water will reveal differences; some, such as

clay, become smooth and easy to apply, while others, such as frits and nepheline syenite, settle quickly and are difficult to handle. This is useful practical information when formulating a glaze.

When fired, the anonymous white and cream coloured powders are transformed, some to a glassy pool spreading across the tile, others to a stiff but molten mass. A few are unaffected by the heat. Differences

between the various firing temperatures will also reveal significant changes. At earthenware temperature only the frits and lithium carbonate will melt, while at high

6   *Two test tiles of glaze materials on stoneware clay. Tile on left shows materials painted on tile before firing. Tile on right shows tile after firing to 1260°C (2300°F) in electric kiln*

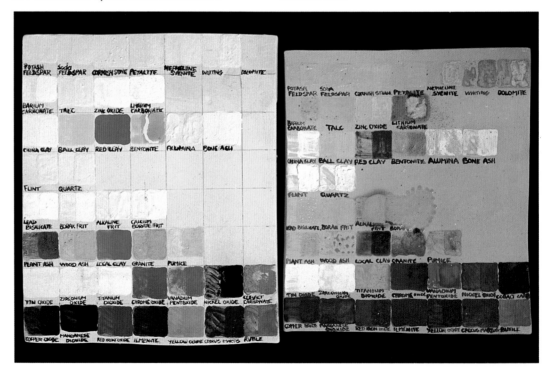

temperature most are affected. The tile fired in an electric kiln will be pale in comparison to the one fired in a reduction atmosphere which will be darker and on the whole display a greater amount of reaction. This is because the lack of oxygen in the atmosphere causes the gases to react more with the clay and glaze so resulting in a fluxing effect bringing out any iron present. In general, the fluxes – whether in the form of frits, single or complex compounds – will have reacted most, while flint and quartz, which have a melting point of around 1730°C (3110°F), will have been little affected and remain as they were when put into the kiln.

## FIRED RESULTS

The reaction between material and body will be affected by the thickness of application. A thinner layer usually has a more powerful reaction than a thicker covering.
**Earthenware** At earthenware temperature few materials are affected: most remain powdery with the exception of the frits which form glassy pools. The red clay and local clay will

7   **James Campbell** – *thrown and turned earthenware dish with slip and painted decoration under clear glaze, about 25 cm (10 in.) across, 1990. Skilled drawing and uncomplicated technique relate this dish to the earthenware tradition in a completely modern way*

have vitrified on the surface of the clay. At this temperature frits are the main fluxes. From the recipes listed in Chapter 7 it is clear that the basis for most earthenware glazes is the lead and borax frits.

**Stoneware** At these temperatures most materials are affected. All the feldspars become glossy and may roll into bead-like opaque balls on the surface of the clay – virtually glazes in their own right. Not all the feldspars behave identically: some will be clearer than others as the small trapped bubbles of air are released. Of all the feldspars, Cornish stone will be least affected.

**Whiting**, which contains calcium, will fuse with the clay to form a yellowish opaque crust, but where thick will be white and powdery. In small quantities whiting is a powerful flux but if used in excess it has the opposite effect, behaving as a refractory.

**Dolomite**, which contains both calcium and magnesium, behaves in a similar fashion to whiting, but in the glaze gives smooth opaque whites.

**Barium carbonate** mostly remains powdery except where it is very thin and fuses with the clay surface. It is a strong flux but is only effective in relatively small quantities; in large amounts it serves as a matting agent. A strong alkaline material, barium carbonate yields bright colours from such oxides as manganese and copper.

**Talc**, like barium carbonate, reacts only slightly with the surface of the clay; it contains magnesium and silica, promoting opaque, silky smooth glazes.

**Zinc oxide** combines with the surface of the clay to give a dry, vitrified surface; it is a powerful flux but if used in large amounts tends to render the glaze opaque and matt. It can also promote the formation of crystals.

**Lithium carbonate** is well-fused on the tile. Being a powerful flux only small amounts are required to be effective.

**Frits** All the frits will have formed glassy pools, some spreading over a wide area, indicating their power as fluxes in the glaze but not their ability to bring different qualities to it.

## AMPHOTERICS

**China clay** has only a limited reaction with the surface of the clay and much of it will have been little affected.

**Ball clay** is reasonably well fused on the surface.

**Red clay** is well vitrified and turns dark brown.

**Bentonite** is fused on the clay.

**Alumina hydrate**, a source of alumina without silica, is unaffected by the heat.

**Bone ash** is little affected and remains as a powder.

## ACIDS

**Flint** and **quartz** are both sources of almost pure silica and are not altered at these temperatures.

## FOUND MATERIALS

**Plant ash and wood ash**, depending on the particular type of plant, will generally fuse on the tile surface to form a yellowish brown matt glaze, similar to whiting. The degree of fusion indicates whether they are soft, and fuse at a lowish temperature, or hard and need a higher temperature.

**Most local clays** will be well fused on the tile.

**Granite** is similar to feldspar but because of the presence of iron is dark coloured.

## COLOURING METAL OXIDES

**Tin oxide, zirconium oxide** and **titanium dioxide** remain as white powders indicating their refractory qualities.

**Chrome oxide** remains as a holly green powder.

**Nickel oxide** remains as a black powder.

**Vanadium pentoxide** remains as a yellow powder.

**Cobalt, copper** and **manganese** all fuse on the clay as black pigments. Their colour is not revealed until they are dissolved in a glaze.

**Iron oxide, yellow ochre, crocus martis**, all forms of iron, become dark brown and fuse on the clay surface.

**Ilmenite** is an ore containing titanium and iron and fuses on the clay.

**Rutile** is a titanium ore which contains small amounts of iron and fuses on the clay.

The fired results indicate the effects of heat on glaze materials, in some cases graphically demonstrating how they can be used. The frits, for example, which form runny pools of glass, would run off a vertical surface and need to be combined with materials to stabilize them. Flint, quartz and China clay, on the other hand, are highly refractory and need to be combined with a powerful flux to make them useful to studio potters. Refractory materials can be made to melt by the presence of a suitable flux, or fluxes. Feldspar, $K_2O.Al_2O_3.6SiO_2$, a naturally occurring mineral, combines all three parts of a glaze: *potassium* ($K_2O$), a flux, *alumina* ($Al_2O_3$), which is an amphoteric or stabilizer, and *silica* ($SiO_2$), the glass former, and fuses at 1260°C (2300°F) to form an opaque, viscous glaze. A stoneware glaze made up only of feldspar will give an opaque, crackly, highly viscous glaze, slow to smooth out on the surface. A glaze made up of equal parts of all the different feldspars results in a smoother surface because the wider range of fluxes react together enhancing their effect. Because such a glaze contains only non-plastic materials, it is difficult to apply and the ingredients settle quickly in the slop to form a hard sediment. The addition of a small amount of clay or bentonite (a highly plastic clay) is needed to keep it in suspension.

Most glazes are made up of two or more materials. A system of discovering how they react when mixed together which indicates the response over all variations can be done simply by blending them in the following proportions:

|  | A | B | C | D | E | F | G | H | I | J | K |
|---|---|---|---|---|---|---|---|---|---|---|---|
| parts of material X | 10 | 9 | 8 | 7 | 6 | 5 | 4 | 3 | 2 | 1 | 0 |
| parts of material Y | 0 | 1 | 2 | 3 | 4 | 5 | 6 | 7 | 8 | 9 | 10 |

| A = | 10 | parts | material X, | no parts | material Y |
|---|---|---|---|---|---|
| B = | 9 | ,, | ,, | 1 | ,, |
| C = | 8 | ,, | ,, | 2 | ,, |
| D = | 7 | ,, | ,, | 3 | ,, |
| E = | 6 | ,, | ,, | 4 | ,, |
| F = | 5 | ,, | ,, | 5 | ,, |
| G = | 4 | ,, | ,, | 6 | ,, |
| H = | 3 | ,, | ,, | 7 | ,, |
| I = | 2 | ,, | ,, | 8 | ,, |
| J = | 1 | ,, | ,, | 9 | ,, |
| K = | 0 | ,, | ,, | 10 | ,, |

The steps are in percentage increases of 10, but if double this number of tests are made the increases are reduced to 5%.

The simplest method is to combine the materials by wet blending, taking spoonsful, or drops of each slop, mixing them thoroughly with a brush and painting them on a tile in a single and a double layer. Write the materials and firing temperature on the tile with manganese dioxide for easy reference. The basic test will indicate areas of useful results; smaller gradations of 5% or less can be carried out for more subtle blends. Suggested combinations for earthenware are lead frit and feldspar, lead frit and any clay. Interesting combinations can also be made by using as one material equal amounts of lead and borax frits combined with equal amounts of feldspar and clay, or clay and flint.

At stoneware temperatures feldspar can be combined with whiting or calcium borate frit. Equally rewarding are combinations of feldspar with iron oxide, wood ash and clay, wood ash and feldspar.

Fascinating though such combinations are in revealing how materials work, in practice they do not always make practical glazes. More than one flux is usually used in a glaze to extend the firing range and make the best use of the qualities of each while a small percentage of clay is needed to keep the glaze slop in suspension and to bind the dry powder on to the pot, making it easier to handle when being packed in the kiln. For glazes which require only a low proportion of alumina, a small amount of bentonite can usually be added without adversely affecting the appearance of the glaze. 2–4% will help deal with the need for a plastic content.

Mixtures of three materials, known as *triaxial blends*, will yield a wide range of useful and attractive glazes, particularly using materials prepared or found yourself, such as wood ash or local clay. Because their composition varies from batch to batch each material has to be tested each time and sufficient has to be collected to make the trial worthwhile. Though more time consuming than line blends, triaxial blends can produce a wide range of workable glazes. The range and variety of results indicates the extent to which different proportions of the same ingredients yield a wide range of glazes.

At *earthenware temperatures* classic combinations are frits, clays and feldspars: Lead bisilicate with China clay and feldspar. Borax frit with China clay and feldspar. Alkaline frit with China clay and feldspar. Two or more frits can be combined to make a single ingredient for more varied results.

At *stoneware temperatures* the possibilities are almost too numerous to list, but the following will yield worthwhile results: Feldspar with dolomite and China clay. Feldspar with whiting and ball clay. Wood ash with feldspar and local clay. Whiting with flint and China clay. Different feldspars will yield different results.

The most efficient method is to wet blend them as described earlier, painting each mixture on a carefully marked out equilateral triangle. The following charts list the system which can be followed.

Ideally a full test should be made. This involves 66 combinations and consists of three tests of single materials, 27 tests of two materials and 36 tests of three materials, as shown:

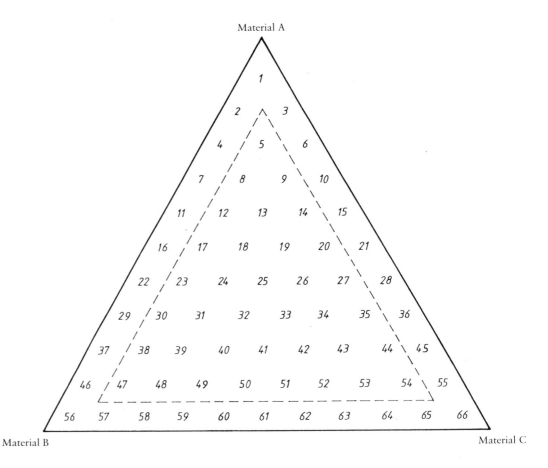

*Triaxial blends: the total number of tests is 66 – omit the biaxial tests to give 36 tests*

| Test no. | % blend | Test no. | % blend | Test no. | % blend | Test no. | % blend | Test no. | % blend | Test no. | % blend |
|---|---|---|---|---|---|---|---|---|---|---|---|
| 1 | 100 A | 14 | 60 A<br>10 B<br>30 C | 26 | 40 A<br>20 B<br>40 C | 38 | 20 A<br>70 B<br>10 C | 49 | 10 A<br>60 B<br>30 C | 62 | 40 B<br>60 C |
| 2 | 90 A<br>10 B | 15 | 60 A<br>40 C | 27 | 40 A<br>10 B<br>50 C | 39 | 20 A<br>60 B<br>20 C | 50 | 10 A<br>50 B<br>40 C | 63 | 30 B<br>70 C |
| 3 | 90 A<br>10 C | 16 | 50 A<br>50 B | 28 | 40 A<br>60 C | 40 | 20 A<br>50 B<br>30 C | 51 | 10 A<br>40 B<br>50 C | 64 | 20 B<br>80 C |
| 4 | 80 A<br>20 B | 17 | 50 A<br>40 B<br>10 C | 29 | 30 A<br>70 B | 41 | 20 A<br>40 B<br>40 C | 52 | 10 A<br>30 B<br>60 C | 65 | 10 B<br>90 C |
| 5 | 80 A<br>10 B<br>10 C | 18 | 50 A<br>30 B<br>20 C | 30 | 30 A<br>60 B<br>10 C | 42 | 20 A<br>30 B<br>50 C | 53 | 10 A<br>20 B<br>70 C | 66 | 100 C |
| 6 | 80 A<br>20 C | 19 | 50 A<br>20 B<br>30 C | 31 | 30 A<br>50 B<br>20 C | 43 | 20 A<br>20 B<br>60 C | 54 | 10 A<br>10 B<br>80 C | | |
| 7 | 70 A<br>30 B | 20 | 50 A<br>10 B<br>40 C | 32 | 30 A<br>40 B<br>30 C | 44 | 20 A<br>10 B<br>70 C | 55 | 10 A<br>90 C | | |
| 8 | 70 A<br>20 B<br>10 C | 21 | 50 A<br>50 C | 33 | 30 A<br>30 B<br>40 C | 45 | 20 A<br>80 C | 56 | 100 B | | |
| 9 | 70 A<br>10 B<br>20 C | 22 | 40 A<br>60 B | 34 | 30 A<br>20 B<br>50 C | 46 | 10 A<br>90 B | 57 | 90 B<br>10 C | | |
| 10 | 70 A<br>30 C | 23 | 40 A<br>50 B<br>10 C | 35 | 30 A<br>10 B<br>60 C | 47 | 10 A<br>80 B<br>10 C | 58 | 80 B<br>20 C | | |
| 11 | 60 A<br>40 B | 24 | 40 A<br>40 B<br>20 C | 36 | 30 A<br>70 C | 48 | 10 A<br>70 B<br>20 C | 59 | 70 B<br>30 C | | |
| 12 | 60 A<br>30 B<br>10 C | 25 | 40 A<br>30 B<br>30 C | 37 | 20 A<br>80 B | | | 60 | 60 B<br>40 C | | |
| 13 | 60 A<br>20 B<br>20 C | | | | | | | | | 61 | 50 B<br>50 C | | |

Triaxial blend of three materials

## Simple triaxial blends of three materials

*A*

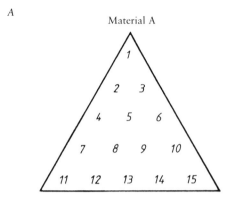

Material A

Material B

Material C

1 = All A
2 = A70 B30
3 = A70 C30
4 = A50 B50
5 = A60 B20 C20
6 = A50 C50
7 = B70 A30

8 = B60 A20 C20
9 = C60 A20 B20
10 = C70 B30
11 = BAll
12 = B70 C30
13 = B50 C50
14 = C70 B30
15 = CAll

NB All tests total 100

*B*

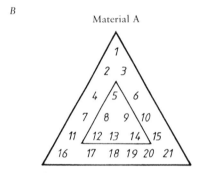

Material A

Material B

Material C

1 All    A = 100
2 A = 80 B = 20
3 A = 80 C = 20
4 A = 60 B = 40
5 A = 60 B = 20 C = 20
6 A = 60 C = 40
7 A = 40 B = 60
8 A = 40 B = 40 C = 20
9 A = 40 B = 20 C = 40
10 A = 40 C = 60

11 A = 20 B = 80
12 A = 20 B = 60 C = 20
13 B = 40 A = 20 C = 40
14 B = 20 A = 20 C = 60
15 A = 20 C = 80
16 B = 100
17 B = 80 C = 20
18 B = 60 C = 40
19 B = 40 C = 60
20 B = 20 C = 80
21 C = 100

Materials such as feldspar and dolomite are complex compounds, while whiting and flint contain only a single active ingredient. Knowledge of the usual amount of a material used in a glaze can suggest more complex blends. For instance two can be used together in one corner of the blend to make a single ingredient. Equal parts of China clay and ball clay can be combined, as can different types of feldspar. Fluxes such as dolomite and barium carbonate can also be intermixed.

The permutations are endless and the results often surprising, especially when the 'rules' are broken.

Scrutinize the fired tiles for possible recipes. If the mixtures have been wet blended then the weight of each material has to be worked out for more accurate testing. The chemical formulae of workable glazes can be calculated following the method outlined in the appendix (page 88). One advantage of using triaxial blends is the visual picture they give as proportions vary. For instance, as the amount of clay increases matt glazes develop while greater amounts of frit will cause the mixture to become too runny.

Tried and tested recipes, homemade mixtures or even ready made combinations will give varying results from potter to potter. Understanding how and why glazes work makes this an easier and more rewarding process.

# CHAPTER TWO

# PREPARING AND MIXING GLAZE

Some potters approach mixing glazes rather like a cook preparing a meal who feels that a bit of this or a pinch of that is required to enhance flavour. Such a method demands a thorough knowledge of ingredients and how they work and, while it may produce good results, it may be difficult or impossible to repeat. Systematic testing and recording not only builds up a body of first hand knowledge but also enables results to be repeated. Though there is often a temptation to add unrecorded and unmeasured ingredients to the glaze, the results can be frustrating when they cannot be reproduced. This chapter describes how to handle, use and adjust glazes, whether purchased ready prepared from suppliers or made up from your own recipes.

A system of recording recipes with any additions made, and annotating them with the results obtained, either in a glaze book or some other system, is invaluable. Some potters prefer reference cards, others a loose leaf glaze book, *Glazo-fax*, which can be added to and rearranged as necessary. Whatever method is used a full record will

8   **Kate Malone** – *bowl, press-moulded with relief decoration, earthenware, about 20 cm (8 in.) tall, 1991. Ingenious use has been made of a basic commercially produced transparent glaze with coloured oxides added giving an attractive liquid quality to the piece*

prevent loss of successful glazes and be a reminder of failures. In practice most potters use only a few glazes and carry out variations on them, but problems do arise. Trying glazes out in different combinations and learning to handle two or three can be more rewarding than moving from glaze to glaze. A record and date of where and when materials are purchased can help sort out any problems which may arise if a regular glaze does not work.

Devise a system of testing which enables results to be compared. Ideally tests should be carried out as closely as possible to the method usually used for glazing. Most studio potters dip or pour glaze, some spray, a few paint. Vertically fired test pieces will indicate how glazes flow and whether they are too runny. Tests fired horizontally will not give this information and any pooling effect may be misleading. Test pieces can be extruded from T-shaped sections chopped into 5 cm (2 in.) lengths, or made from wedges cut from leatherhard thrown flat dishes. The simplest are clay tiles about 7·5 cm × 5 cm (3 in. × 2 in.) fired propped on suitable stands. A hole pierced in them when leatherhard enables the tiles to be conveniently mounted for easy reference. Test pieces need to be sufficiently large to indicate the colour and texture of a glaze with an incised pattern to show how it will break.

In flame-burning kilns test rings are particularly useful as they can be lifted out during firing to indicate how the glaze is progressing. They can be simply made by rolling out and flattening lengths of clay about 7·5 cm (3 in.) long, wrapping them round to form a circle, or pressed to form a flat base to stand upright. They can be hooked from the kiln during the firing.

Glazes can be conveniently tested in batches of 100 grams ($3\frac{1}{2}$ oz). Ideally all recipes should total 100 with the ingredients expressed as percentage parts. This enables quick comparisons to be made with other glazes and any additions to be seen easily. Such proportions can conveniently be translated into larger amounts if the recipe is to be made into a batch.

Calculating the glaze to total 100 is relatively straightforward, particularly with a pocket calculator. Omitting any additions to the base glaze, add up the ingredients then divide each individual amount by this total and multiply by 100. Results can be rounded off to the nearest whole number. Any colouring or opacifying additions can be expressed as a percentage over and above this. The following glaze, a smooth white, firing at 1260°C (2300°F), serves as an example:

| | |
|---|---|
| Feldspar | 30 |
| Cornish stone (Cornwall stone) | 10 |
| Whiting | 5 |
| Dolomite | 30 |
| China clay | 20 |
| Ball clay | 15 |
| | 110 |

To express the ingredients in percentages, each of the figures is divided by the total of 110 and multiplied by 100, ie

$$\text{Feldspar } \frac{30 \times 100}{110} = 27.$$

When all the calculations have been carried out the recipe now reads to whole numbers:

| | |
|---|---|
| Feldspar | 27 |
| Cornish stone (Cornwall stone) | 9 |
| Whiting | 4 |
| Dolomite | 27 |
| China clay | 19 |
| Ball clay | 14 |

Tin oxide 8% will make the glaze whiter, an amount simply expressed as an addition to the full percentage.

Test batches totalling 100 grams ($3\frac{1}{2}$ oz) fit conveniently a 227 grams (8 oz) sized plastic beaker. These cups can be reclaimed from canteens, or purchased cheaply from catering suppliers together with lids. Suitable suppliers are usually listed in the telephone directory under *Disposables*. All beakers need to be clearly marked with, say, a felt tipped pen to avoid the possibility of accidental confusion over the contents. This is particularly important in educational establishments and shared workshops where health and safety regulations are stringently applied to prevent accidentally consuming the contents in mistake for a beverage. Unlabelled beakers also represent wasted materials.

For larger batches of glaze the percentage proportions can conveniently be multiplied. A domestic bucket will hold some 3000 grams while for potters measuring in pounds and ounces a bucket of glaze can be translated as 100 oz and duly rendered in pounds and ounces. The glaze listed earlier serves as an example:

| | % | gram batch (× 3) | lb | oz |
|---|---|---|---|---|
| Feldspar | 27 | 81 | 1 | 11 |
| Cornish stone (Cornwall stone) | 9 | 27 | — | 9 |
| Whiting | 4 | 12 | — | 4 |
| Dolomite | 27 | 81 | 1 | 11 |
| China clay | 19 | 57 | 1 | 3 |
| Ball clay | 14 | 42 | — | 14 |

# MIXING GLAZE

Glaze purchased ready prepared, usually as powder, need only be mixed with water and sieved to make it ready for use. Always slide, never drop, glaze materials in water to reduce dust, and add powder to water rather than the other way round as this can cause hard lumps to form. Leave to slake or soak down before stirring thoroughly. Pass the liquid twice through an 80s mesh sieve to yield a smooth homogeneous mix. Brush-on glazes now sold by many suppliers are already in liquid form and need no sieving before use. Keep lids well screwed on to prevent them drying out. Follow manufacturers' instructions.

**Preparing glazes** Weigh out each ingredient carefully (this is particularly important for small quantities) and gently add them to more water than is needed for the final mix. Hot water will speed up the mixing process.

Accurate weighing is essential, especially for small test batches when a chemical balance is ideal. A range of precise and accurate balances is now on the market and it is worth investing in a good one. For larger amounts high quality balance scales are best as long as the pivot is not worn. Spring scales are rarely sufficiently accurate, particularly for small quantities.

Tick off each ingredient as it is weighed and added. This will help prevent mistakes especially if you are interrupted. Leave the mixture to slake and break down, then mix thoroughly by hand, paddle or mechanical mixer until smooth. Using an excess of water will make this easier. Pass the mixture through a 60s then a 100s mesh sieve, gently agitating the mixture in the sieve. Repeat this

if lumps are present. Most materials should pass through the sieve without difficulty, and any coarse particles which remain can be discarded.

Excess of water aids sieving, but then time has to be allowed for the glaze to settle so surplus water can be removed if the consistency is too thin. It is good practice when mixing up a prepared but settled glaze to remove more water than is necessary as this can easily be replaced once the ingredients have been well stirred. Most glazes need to be the thickness of single cream, but some are better thicker, others thinner. Lastly, clearly label the bucket or container with the description and even the recipe of the glaze. The glaze can be tested on a clearly labelled circular tile which can be attached to the container as an effective visual record of the contents. A well fitting lid on the glaze bucket will keep out foreign bodies and also help prevent it drying out. Plastic containers are ideal. They are light in weight and tend not to be affected by the glaze contents, while their smooth surface is easily wiped clean with a rubber kidney.

# WOOD ASH AND LOCAL CLAYS

Most glazes can be safely kept over time and if they dry out can be slaked down without any noticeable change in quality. A few materials are slightly soluble in water and

9 **Jim Malone** – *stoneware bottle, wheel thrown with ash glaze fired in reduction, 25 cm (10 in.) tall, 1987. The runny glaze is characteristic of ash glazes and here is sensitively related to the bottle form*

*10* **Harry Horlock Stringer** – *bowl with runny ash-type glaze, thrown and turned stoneware, electric kiln, about 254 mm (10 in.) across, c 1985. The movement of the glaze enlivens the classic form of this stoneware bowl and reveals the incised decoration*

through a coarse mesh. The ash will contain soluble salts and the batch will change with time.

Washed wood ash is a more reliable glaze material. The ash is first placed in an excess of water, vigorously stirred and left to soak for a day or two. The soluble salts will turn the water pale yellow, making it feel soapy to the touch and, being strongly alkaline, will be slightly corrosive. Remove, replace with fresh water and vigorously stir again. Repeat three or four times until the water is clear then sieve with plenty of water through an 80s mesh sieve (or finer), allow to settle, remove the water and allow the ash to dry.

Wood or plant ashes are particularly effective glaze ingredients at stoneware temperatures when the drama of the material with its complex structure will produce thin, slightly runny glazes which respond to the iron in the clay and enhance and heighten the form of the pot. In electric kilns greater quantities of wood ash are required to achieve effects similar to reduction though the effects can be equally attractive.

Like wood ash, local clays can yield rich and unusual glazes. Suitable clays are found beneath soil about a metre below the surface, or deposited as silt on the bottom of ponds or rivers. To prepare the clay allow it to dry out, say, on top of the kiln, break in small lumps and add to an excess of water. Sieve through a 60s or 100s mesh sieve to remove any small stones and give a homogeneous mix. Allow the liquid to settle (which may

may change over time. This is particularly noticeable when using local materials. Wood ash in particular contains quantities of soluble salts which can either be washed out or left as an integral part of the material. Ash collected from fire-grates or bonfires may contain such assorted materials as charcoal, small stones and other extraneous matter which can be removed by careful sieving take a few days because of the fine particle size of the clay), dry the clay out and break it into small lumps ready for use. Local clays, which usually contain iron, are excellent for use in iron bearing glazes.

# ADJUSTING AND DEVELOPING THE GLAZE

Unlike the ceramic industry, studio potters rarely want glazes in which all chemical ingredients are perfectly balanced. For studio potters the quality of a glaze may depend on it containing an excess of some ingredient, placing it on the edge of being useful at all. So the conventional rules for adjusting and altering glazes must be related to the particular needs of individual studio potters. However, potters are not free of responsibility when using glaze. Functional pots, for example, require a surface which is safe in that it must not be affected by the food or drink with which it comes into contact, as well as being smooth to use, hygienic and attractive. Such glazes must also fit the body and be compatible with it, as this not only prevents crazing but strengthens the pot making it more resistant to cracking and chipping.

**Crazing** An ideal fit between body and glaze is one where the glaze is in slight compression and the body has shrunk slightly more than the glaze. This sets up a tension which physically makes the pot stronger. To be successful the body must be reasonably well vitrified or it will absorb moisture, eventually causing the glaze to craze. Under-vitrified bodies usually lack strength, a fault not remedied by glaze, which may cause the pot to split apart.

Scaling or flaking is the opposite of crazing and occurs when the compression of the glaze is too great, literally forcing it off edges of handles or rims of pots as thin slivers of glaze, a dangerous fault particularly for functional work.

Some crazed glazes, known as *crackle* or *cracquelle*, are thought to be attractive, a quality admired for their decorative qualities particularly if the crackle is stained, making it a feature of the pot. Crazed or cracquelled glazes are not well-fitting and if tapped will result in a dull thud rather than an echoing ping. Because the craze or crackle is literally made up of numerous hair-line cracks in the surface such glazes should be avoided on pots intended for domestic use because liquid can penetrate the surface which is difficult if not impossible to wash out, and so are unhygienic. Refiring will burn out any organic material but may affect the glaze.

Potters therefore may want to solve the problem of crazing when a well fitting glaze is required, or seek to make an attractive crackle surface for more decorative ware. Though the theory of body-glaze fit is well understood, faults may be difficult to remedy. A glaze which crazes and contracts more than the body requires either the addition of a

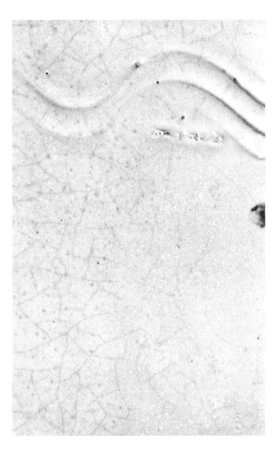

11 *A smooth crackled stoneware glaze over porcelain, more crackled where it is more thickly applied, electric kiln.* RECIPE: *soda feldspar 60, whiting 7, dolomite 13, China clay 20*

material such as silica, in the form of flint to the glaze in amounts of up to 6–8%, or the addition or substitution of a flux such as boric oxide (added as borax frit) or zinc oxide, which have a low level of expansion and contraction. Fluxes which need to be restricted are alkalies such as potassium and sodium which expand and contract greatly. Increasing or lowering the firing temperature may also help by causing a greater or lesser degree of melt. Changing the thickness of glaze application will also affect this: the thicker it is, the more likely it is to craze.

Crackle glazes make use of fluxes which have a high level of contraction such as potassium and sodium, present in feldspars and alkaline frits. The difficulty is to achieve a smooth surface as well as one which has crackled. A useful starting point for a stoneware crackle glaze is Cornish stone 85, whiting 12, dolomite 2 plus bentonite 2. This glaze gives a smooth satin white at 1260°C–1270°C (2300°F–2318°F) and can be stained by rubbing finely ground pigments such as artists' gouache or Chinese ink into the glaze surface. The pigment may enter the crackle more effectively if the pot is heated to around 200°C (380°F), when the pot expands slightly,

12  **David Leach** – *bottle form with two lidded boxes, thrown and turned porcelain with matt crackle glaze, about 20 cm (8 in.), 1980. The crackle in the matt glaze has been highlighted by rubbing in iron pigment to create a pleasing decorative effect*

opening up the lines. At this temperature water based pigments dry almost instantly and perseverance is required. Oil based pigments may be an alternative.

Crackle and crazing are elusive. While in theory they are not difficult either to obtain or remedy, in practice glaze may resist any attempt to move in one direction or the other, and may require subtle changes.

**Blistering and bubbling** Blistered or bubbled glazes usually indicate overfiring, or, more rarely, incompatibility between body and glaze. During firing the glaze ingredients react giving off gases and steam in quite large quantities. As the temperature rises the reaction may become more violent and the glaze may boil and bubble until fully melted. Sufficient time is needed for it to settle and to enable any bubbling to subside and smooth over. If the temperature continues to rise, the reactions continue and the fluxes become

*13 (Top)* **Brian Bevan** – *bowl, porcelain thrown and turned with semi-matt opaque crackle glaze, reduction fired, 15 cm (6 in.) across, 1982. Based on a classic Chinese Guan bowl, the unctuous crackle glaze was achieved by very thick applications of a glaze made up of Cornish stone 85, whiting 15, ball clay 10, bentonite 3, yellow ochre 1*

*14  Stoneware bowl with one glaze applied over another with which it is incompatible resulting in huge blisters of glaze. Grinding and refiring will resolve the problem*

volatile and burn away leaving a blistered and burnt looking surface. The obvious solution is to avoid such occurrence. Lower the firing temperature and ensure there is sufficient time for the glaze to fully mature. An overfired pot can often be saved by re-glazing. First heat the pot and apply a layer of glaze mixed with a little gum arabic to make it adhere to the vitrified surface. Refire slowly. Incompatible glaze and body can be separated by a layer of slip to act as a buffer between them.

**Dry, dull surfaces** These may be the opposite of over firing. Perhaps insufficient time has been allowed for the glaze and body to mature, the firing temperature is too low or the glaze has been put on too thinly. The solution is either to fire to a higher temperature or increase the length of firing so that there is more time for maturation to take place. The firing temperature of the glaze can be lowered either by increasing the fluxes or decreasing the silica and clay content. The addition of a small quantity (5–8%) of a powerful flux such as calcium borate frit can also lower the firing temperature without drastically altering the quality of the glaze. Badly constructed glazes may never form a proper layer and may need to be re-thought to make them work well.

**Crawling** Like crazing, crawling can be regarded as a decorative effect or as an unsightly blemish – particularly on functional ware. Crawling occurs when the glaze rolls into beads, leaving bald patches. A common

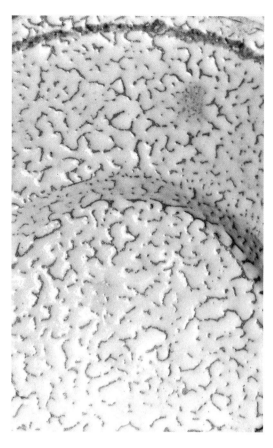

15  *Stoneware saucer (detail) showing a crawled glaze surface caused by an excess of zinc oxide in the recipe for this tin glaze; a remedy is to apply the glaze more thinly and to ensure it is well sieved before use*

cause is where the glaze has not adhered to the surface because it is too high in plastic ingredients, has been applied too thickly or over a layer of dry materials such as underglaze colour. Glazes high in plastic materials, such as ball or China clay and thickly applied, may crack into small islands during drying which do not heal over and join up in the firing leaving a crawled appearance. The remedy is to replace some of the plastic clay by calcined clay which does not shrink as it dries.

Glazes high in opacifying materials or matting agents such as tin oxide, zirconium oxide or titanium oxide which are highly refractory can also cause crawling. Careful application is need to avoid over-wetting the pot while the addition of a small amount of flux to the glaze may make it more fluid and solve the problem. At the same time this may reduce opacity necessitating a thicker application of glaze. Saturation of the pot by leaving it too long in the glaze slop can be another cause of crawling. Avoid this by glazing the inside and allowing this to dry before covering the outside. The most popular method of inducing crawling is to load the glaze with highly plastic materials such as ball or China clay, but like crackle, it can be an elusive effect.

**Matt glazes** An excess of one or more ingredients in the glaze is the simplest way to make glazes matt. From the scientific point of view a perfect glaze has all the chemical constituents in balance, with sufficient flux,

alumina and silica to create a smooth, transparent covering which fits the body tightly. While practical and hygienic, such glazes are likely to add little to the aesthetic appeal of the pot. Shiny glazes, sometimes known as wet glazes, reflect light, thus breaking up the surface and visually affecting or even destroying the form. Matt glazes absorb light and tend to enhance shape. Satin glazes, halfway between matt and shiny, are often an attractive compromise for pots intended for use.

Matt glazes have their own qualities. They should not be confused with opaque glazes which have an opacifier suspended in the fired glaze, nor are they underfired as are all the chemical ingredients in a well fused glaze. Shiny or satin glazes which fire matt may just be underfired. Matt glazes are a form of super-saturated liquid and contain an excess of one material which at top temperature goes into solution. During cooling they form a fine network of crystals invisible to the naked eye, save for their overall effect. In crystalline glazes the crystals are large and visible. Matt glazes appear smooth, though under a powerful hand lens the surface will appear uneven and slightly pitted. A well formed matt glaze has a surface which is hygienic and non-staining.

16   **Gordon Baldwin** – *handbuilt vessel form with incised decoration, high-fired, about 38 cm (15 in.) tall, 1990. The use of a matt glaze effectively brings out the subtlety of the form*

The rate of cooling of the kiln plays a vital part in achieving matt surfaces. Too rapid a drop in temperature once the highest point has been reached does not allow sufficient time for the crystalline structure to form. Industrial firings aim for rapid cooling to ensure the glazes stay clear and bright, but most studio potters want slow cooling and leave kilns to cool at their own rate. Temperature fall can be controlled by an input of heat either by a low flame or, in electric kilns, by turning on the power. Matt glazes, as described earlier, are related to crystalline glazes where the cooling cycle is crucial to the formation of crystals. During the cooling the temperature is held for a couple of hours to allow crystals to form in the glaze matrix. Crystalline glaze effects are described in Chapter 7.

Glazes high in *zinc*, *alumina* or *alkaline* earths such as calcium (present in whiting) and barium, are three major sorts of matt effects and may be used in conjunction with each other. Quite simply, increasing additions to a clear glaze of zinc oxide, China clay, whiting or barium carbonate will result in a wide range of matt glazes. This effect can quickly be demonstrated by a line blend of a transparent glaze and one of these materials. Commercial matting agents can be used in

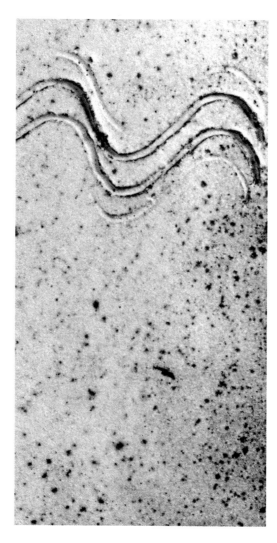

the same way and are effective over a wide temperature range. They can be made by calcining together equal parts of zinc oxide and China clay at 950°C (1742°F) then grinding it to a fine powder. Matting agents, whether purchased ready made or produced in the studio, are particularly effective in earthenware glazes where they can give smooth, silky surfaces. The quantity required needs to be determined by a line blend, the usual amount ranging from 5–15%.

*17 A dry matt stoneware glaze responding to the iron speckle in the clay body.* RECIPE: *feldspar 62, whiting 12, dolomite 13, China clay 13 + tin oxide 7.5%*

*18 (Right)* **Ruth Duckworth** *– handbuilt high-fired porcelain sculptural form, 20 cm (8 in.) tall. The qualities of this powerful piece are brought out well by this matt white glaze with delicate iron specking*

*19 (Far right)* **Alison Britton** *–* Brown Torso Pot *with checks, handbuilt, high-fired earthenware, painted with slip and underglaze pigment, 43 cm (17 in.) tall, c 1985. The smooth matt clear glaze and the energetic decoration on this sculptural form imaginatively combines freedom with control*

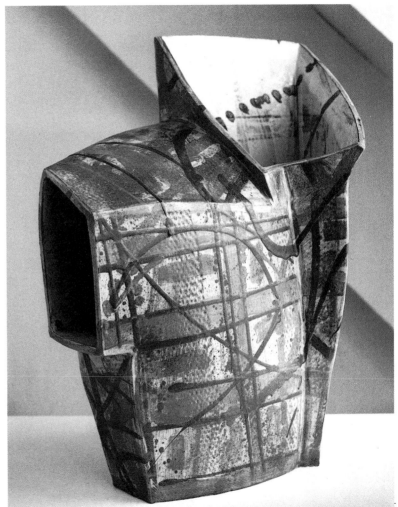

# CHAPTER THREE

# COLOURING THE GLAZE

Over the last twenty years there has been a minor revolution in the use of colour in glazes as new technology has made a wider range available. Taste too has changed. The subtle but muted greys, pale greens and browns of stoneware fired in a reduction atmosphere have given way to a range of bright rich colours including blues, pinks, yellows and oranges, especially in electric kilns. Reduction-fired stonewares, characterized by speckled bodies and colours derived from iron, can be beautiful and subtle. But the widespread interest in ceramics of the Far East, advocated by Bernard Leach and his followers in the 1960s and '70s, became less popular in the 1980s as potters freely explored other influences. The extended palette offers the challenge of using colour well and the opportunity to explore a wide range of pleasing and cheerful effects so that pot and glaze remain in harmony. The availability of technical information and a good variety of prepared colours offer many opportunities for experiment.

Colour in glaze derives mainly from metal oxides, used either in their basic raw state or

20  **Takeshi Yasuda** – Bucket Form, *thrown stoneware with iron and manganese decoration under gold honey glaze, 35 cm (14 in.) tall, 1987. Effective use is made of a basic clear glaze with oxide colour to create a classical effect*

in the form of commercially produced stains. They can be either introduced in the glaze or incorporated in slips applied under the glaze, a system which also serves as a buffer layer between them. The use of slips is discussed in detail in Chapter 5.

## METAL COLOURING OXIDES

Metal oxides work either by going into solution and staining the glaze or by suspending themselves in it. Oxides which go into solution allow light to pass through, while oxides which suspend themselves in the glaze matrix are refractory and reflect and refract light. The way an oxide works depends not only on the particular oxide but also on the amount used; even with the most refractory oxides a small percentage goes into solution giving subtle but beautiful results. If added in excess, soluble oxides will render glaze opaque and may turn it matt.

**Iron oxide**, ($Fe_2O_3$), is one of the commonest oxides. Iron is present in small quantities in most ceramic materials. Red clay contains about 8%. Iron is usually added to glazes in the form of red iron oxide which gives colours ranging from pale blues and greens (in reduction atmospheres) to rich tenmokus. In electric kilns colours extend from pale creams, yellows and olives to blacks and opaque red-browns. Percentage additions range from 0.5%–15%. Depending on the type of glaze up to about 10% of iron will go into solution. Amounts above this are likely to cause the glaze to become saturated and opaque colours will result. Synthetic red iron oxide ($Fe_2O_3$) is the purest and most reliable in composition and, weight for weight, most powerful. Natural red iron oxide contains varying amounts of clay and may muddy the colour. Black iron oxide behaves in a similar way to red.

The amount of iron oxide and type of glaze are crucial to the results achieved. In a clear glaze, fluxed mainly by calcium, typical colours are pale blues to soft greens (1%), olive greens (4%), tenmoku/black (8–9%) to tea dust (12–15%). In matt glazes with dolomite or barium carbonate muddy dull coffee-browns result. In clear glazes which contain 8–10% bone ash, 8–12% iron oxide gives bright copper-red browns which can break to an attractive mottle.

**Crocus martis**, ($FeSO_4$), is a naturally occurring form of iron oxide which has the advantage of being partly soluble in water. At lower temperatures it gives yellows and greens, while at stoneware temperature in the

*21* **Bernard Leach** – *press-moulded bottle, reduction fired stoneware, 37.7 cm (14½ in.) tall, 1970. The rich deep tenmoku breaks to light gold on edges bringing out the strength and majesty of this classic shape*

*22* **David Leach** – *stoneware bottle form, thrown and turned, rich dark brown tenmoku glaze and painted iron decoration, 30 cm (12 in.) tall, reduction fired, 1980. Where the iron saturates the glaze it turns a bright orange*

electric kiln it can result in lively red-browns. **Red and yellow ochre** are naturally occurring earths, variable in composition with a high proportion of iron oxide combined with fine particled clay, giving subtle shades when added in tiny quantities to glaze. If used in larger amounts of up to 25% or more they serve as a major part of the glaze, replacing clay. Some ochres melt and flow at stoneware temperatures on the clay surface when applied on their own while others are more refractory. For these reasons each batch of ochre has to be tested before use. Intense red-browns can be obtained by blending feldspar with ochre.

**Ilmenite**, $(FeO.TiO_2)$, is a combination of titanium and iron which tends to give speckles in the glaze. If used for in-glaze decoration, painted on top of the unfired glaze, attractive yellows, browns and blacks can be obtained.

**Rutile**, $(TiO_2)$, is a naturally occurring form of titanium dioxide with a small amount of iron. It is available as light, medium or dark indicating the amount of iron present. Rutile

*23 (Opposite)   Test tiles of various glazes all fired to stoneware temperature*

TOP ROW *left to right*
(A) *Chrome pink stoneware glaze (Cornish stone 50, whiting 30, flint 5, China clay 15) + tin oxide 5% and chrome oxide 0.1%, reduction*
(B) *Same glaze and colour addition fired in electric kiln*
(C) *Barium matt glaze (feldspar 55, dolomite 5, barium carbonate 20, flint 10, China clay 10) fired in reduction*
(D) *+ cobalt carbonate 1%, electric kiln*
(E) *+ copper carbonate 2%, reduction*
(F) *+ copper carbonate 2%, electric kiln*
(G) *Transparent stoneware glaze, (Cornish stone 50, whiting 20, flint 15, China clay 15) + cobalt carbonate 0.75% and manganese carbonate 2%, electric kiln*
(H) *+ copper carbonate 2.5%, electric kiln*

SECOND ROW *left to right*
(A) *Smooth stoneware glaze (feldspar 48, whiting 16, talc 8, zinc oxide 3, flint 24, China clay 5) + cobalt carbonate 1%, electric kiln*
(B) *+ copper carbonate 3%, electric kiln*
(C) *+ tin oxide 8%, electric kiln*
(D) *+ zinc oxide 2%, electric kiln*
(E) *+ zinc oxide 2% over stoneware body, electric kiln*
(F) *+ manganese carbonate 4%, electric kiln*
(G) *Transparent stoneware glaze (Cornish stone 50, whiting 20, flint 15, China clay 15) fired in reduction*
(H) *+ red iron oxide 4, reduction*

THIRD ROW *left to right*
(A) *Matt alkaline glaze (nepheline syenite 55, barium carbonate 25, lithium carbonate 2, flint 8, China clay 6) + tin oxide 6%, electric kiln, stoneware clay*
(B) *+ tin oxide 9%, electric kiln, porcelain*
(C) *+ chrome oxide 0.5%, electric kiln*
(D) *+ rutile 8%, electric kiln*
(E) *+ manganese 4%, electric kiln*
(F) *+ copper carbonate 3%, electric kiln*
(G) *Matt barium zinc glaze (feldspar 35, flint 5, barium carbonate 30, zinc oxide 25, China clay 15) + nickel oxide 1.5%, electric kiln*
(H) *Dry barium zinc glaze (feldspar 35, flint 5, barium carbonate 40, zinc oxide 15, China clay 15) + nickel oxide 3%, electric kiln*

BOTTOM ROW *left to right*
(A) *Clear stoneware glaze (nepheline syenite 35, dolomite 15, whiting 5, China clay 9, flint 33, zinc oxide 3) + copper carbonate 2, reduction*
(B) *+ copper carbonate 2%, electric kiln*
(C) *Smooth matt stoneware glaze (nepheline syenite 35, dolomite 20, whiting 5, China clay 20, flint 20) + copper carbonate 1.5%, electric kiln*
(D) *+ copper carbonate 1.5%, reduction*
(E) *Dry barium matt stoneware glaze (nepheline syenite 55, dolomite 5, barium carbonate 20, flint 10, China clay 10) + cobalt carbonate 0.5% and manganese dioxide 1%, electric kiln, showing effect of double thickness, porcelain*
(F) *Same glaze and colour additions fired over dark stoneware clay in reduction*
(G) *Soft pink glaze (soda feldspar 62, whiting 28, China clay 10 + tin oxide 8%) fired in electric kiln where the glaze has picked up chrome pink flashing*
(H) *+ tin oxide 6% and chrome oxide 0.1%, electric kiln*

depends for its effects on the make up of the glaze. In some glazes 3–8% will give yellows and pale browns and cause the surface to break up into a mottled texture if fired horizontally. Greater amounts of rutile (up to 25%) can help cause crystallization in the glaze matrix yielding pinks and oranges. In glazes containing calcium borate frit (or gerstley borate) rutile will go into solution breaking down to give optical blues with cream streaks. The effect can be dramatic but is sensitive to temperature. 1–2% rutile can have an attractive softening effect on other colouring oxides.

**Copper** is used as copper oxide (CuO) or copper carbonate ($CuCO_3$), and occasionally in the form of cuprous oxide ($Cu_2O$). In quantities of 1–4% copper will usually give a variety of greens in electric kilns over a wide temperature range. In some glazes this versatile oxide will yield a wide range of colours from salmon pinks and greys, apple greens and turquoise blues in electric kilns, to peach bloom and rich deep reds, *rouge flambé*, in reduction. Copper starts to become volatile around 1050°C–1100°C (1922°F–2012°F) but remains active in glazes over the whole temperature range. It is an active flux

*24* **Philip Cornelius** – Winchester, *handbuilt porcelain teapot with satin-green glaze, about 35 cm (14 in.) tall, 1989. The semi-transparent glaze brings out the strength of the form by running off edges enhancing the structure of the teapot*

and will form a matt black pewter-like pigment on the surface of clay at around 1100°C (2012°F). The quantity of copper used, the make up of the glaze and the atmosphere in which it is fired are crucial to the colours obtained. Over 4–5% causes an excess in many glazes resulting in a matt pewter-like black. Copper oxide is black in colour and weight for weight is more powerful than the carbonate. The carbonate, usually green in colour, is less strong but has a smaller particle size. Cuprous oxide, dark red in colour, is rarely used because it is more difficult to mix with water. Some potters prefer this form for use in reduction firing to obtain pinks and reds. Finely ground copper metal can also be used for its decorative effect.

Copper is best known for producing green. At earthenware temperatures in alkaline or borax glazes it gives varying shades of turquoise and mid-greens. Its use in lead glazes has almost ceased due to its ability to render lead in a more soluble form and hence is poisonous. In properly formulated and balanced glazes lead and copper can be used safely together but it is a wise precaution to avoid such glazes for functional pots. Similar shades can be obtained by using tiny proportions of chrome in lead glazes.

At stoneware temperatures calcium glazes will produce apple-greens in electric kilns. These reliable colours are transparent and depend on the colour of the clay body for their depth. Brighter shades require a lighter coloured body. In electric kilns, in glazes high in magnesium (particularly dolomite), 1–2% copper will produce salmon pinks and greys. The colour can be fickle and is not always dependable. Glazes high in alkaline fluxes such as barium carbonate, nepheline syenite and lithium carbonate give rich matt turquoise blues over light coloured bodies or porcelain. Though the colours of such mixtures are perfectly reliable, because the glaze is matt it needs to be applied evenly as it remains highly viscous even at top temperature.

In reduction firings copper changes from its green to its red state. In electric kilns this can be achieved with small quantities of silicon carbide (0.5–2%) in glazes containing such powerful fluxes as calcium borate frit (or gerstley borate) or borax frit. During the firing the silicon carbide breaks down and has a reducing effect on the copper, turning it red. A small amount of tin oxide (2%) helps the colour to form. Some 1–2% of copper is needed. Such glazes need to become quite fluid to ensure their success at breaking down the silicon carbide and may become runny, hence caution is needed in their application.

Copper glazes in reduction atmospheres offer a unique spectrum of subtle colours ranging from deep reds and purples to mottled pink and orange known as peach bloom. The Chinese were the first to develop such effects and their results have rarely been bettered. Such glazes depend on the composition of the glaze and on the degree and length of reduction. Some potters start reduction at an early point in the firing using glazes which melt and trap the copper, maintaining reduction until top temperature is reached. Firing cycles are described in Chapter 6. The presence of a small amount of borax frit encourages the glaze to melt. 1–2% of tin oxide is conducive to the formation of colour as is 1–2% iron oxide. Barium carbonate in amounts of 5–10% will help hold the colour. As copper is volatilized and released as a gas, it can be picked up by glazes in the kiln sensitive to it and which may be made or marred by pink blushes of colour.

**Manganese** is available as manganese dioxide ($MnO_2$), a black powder, and as manganese carbonate ($MnCO_2$) which is coffee coloured. Weight for weight the dioxide is stronger than the carbonate. In glazes and slips manganese yields browns and blacks but in alkaline bases it produces purples and violets. Manganese is particularly useful for softening the colour of other oxides. A powerful flux, manganese will fire on the clay at 1080°C (1976°F) as a black pigment. In earthenware glazes 2–10% manganese in alkaline glazes will produce pale creams to purple browns. It is probably most useful in combination with iron oxide when the two give a rich Rockingham brown – manganese dioxide 4%, iron oxide 7%. In conjunction with iron oxide (5%), and cobalt oxide (2%), manganese dioxide (4%) will give attractive blacks.

At stoneware temperature 2–4%
manganese will give attractive soft mauves
and purples in alkaline glazes such as those
containing barium carbonate and nepheline
syenite. Used on its own or, to make it easier
to handle, with small amounts of clay,
manganese will give reliable, smooth, slightly
textured black-brown pigment glazes. These
are excellent for enhancing form though the
matt, slightly pitted surface, is not
recommended for functional vessels.
Combinations of copper one part and
manganese seven parts will give gold-bronze
effects at medium to high stoneware
temperatures. This pigment is easier to apply
if combined with a small percentage of red
clay or China clay.

**Cobalt** is used as cobalt oxide (CoO), which
is black, and cobalt carbonate ($CoCO_3$)
which is usually a pale purple colour. The
oxide is stronger than the carbonate but tends

*25 (Right)* **Eileen Lewenstein** – Standing
Forms, *handbuilt using grogged clay, high-
fired stoneware with high whiting and clay
glaze stained with cobalt and iron, 41 cm (16
in.) tall, 1990. The richly coloured textured
glaze is well suited to the flat sides of the
curving form*

*26 (Left)* **Emmanuel Cooper** – *thrown and
turned high-fired porcelain bowl, turquoise
glaze over slip containing 2% silicon carbide,
28 cm (11 in.) across, 1990. A simple bowl
form enhanced by the textured glaze*

to speckle in glazes unless finely ground. The carbonate is easier to use without this problem. As one of the most powerful oxides giving typical 'cobalt' blues and mauves, cobalt needs to be handled sensitively; small amounts will contaminate glazes and even the slightest finger-mark bearing a trace of cobalt can result in unsightly blue smudges.

Cobalt is most closely associated with the blue and white wares of China, particularly of the Ming dynasty, where it was skilfully painted over large areas of decoration. The range of blues indicates that the cobalt was mixed with other oxides. Combined with equal parts of manganese, cobalt becomes greyer and the colour more subtle. Other shades can be obtained with different oxides.

Consistent and effective over the entire temperature range and under different firing conditions, cobalt readily goes into solution in the glaze and is a reliable source of blue. In fully fluxed glazes 0.5% is all that is usually required to produce a strong dark blue. Matt glazes may require greater amounts but rarely more than 1–2%. The intensity of the blue can be heightened by the addition of a small percentage of zinc oxide (2–3%) which encourages deeper shades. Subtle effects can be achieved in glazes containing magnesium in the form of dolomite, talc or magnesium carbonate, which turn cobalt shades of mauve and violet.

Because cobalt is so powerful, it is not always easy to add it in sufficiently small quantities to bring out its subtle effects. Using the carbonate helps but an alternative is to prepare a 'cobalt mix' made up of a combination of cobalt one part and China clay nine parts. Wet ground, passed through a fine mesh and dried, it can be used instead of the pure oxide. Cobalt is particularly attractive if used in tiny quantities in conjunction with such oxides as copper, manganese, nickel and chromium, to obtain delicate and subtle shades of blue and green.

**Chrome** Chrome oxide ($Cr_2O_3$) is a holly green coloured powder which in most glazes gives a shade very similar to that of the raw oxide. Only small amounts are required (0.5–2%) in transparent glazes where the oxide suspends itself in the glaze turning it an opaque and evenly coloured green. Such a smooth coating, masking any reaction from the body even in reduction, can result in dull, lifeless glazes. If used in very small amounts or in combinations with tiny proportions of oxides, such as cobalt and copper, subtle shades can be obtained.

The colours yielded by chrome are affected by the quantity used, the firing temperature and composition of the glaze. In glazes containing zinc, chrome is turned shades of brown, but in zinc-free transparent glazes tiny amounts of chrome (0.25%) with 6–8% of tin oxide will result in attractive pinks and crimson reds. Small amounts of chrome volatilize, attaching themselves to tin as a pink or red pigment. In such small quantities chrome can be elusive, particularly at stoneware temperatures when the volatile material can give its most subtle effects but can also burn away with too much heat.

In low temperature lead glazes, chrome gives a range of bright colours though they cannot under any circumstances be used for bearing food. In high lead, low alumina glazes 2–3% of chrome can produce reds, yellows and oranges in mottled and textured surfaces. While brightly coloured and highly decorative, such glazes are saturated with lead to produce the colour and hence cannot be considered functional surfaces. Raw lead in the form of lead oxide gives the strongest reds, but as this is highly poisonous its use is not recommended. A lead frit, such as lead monosilicate, may be substituted; it is safe to handle but must not be thought suitable for functional surfaces. Typical recipes are made up of lead monosilicate 93, feldspar 3, China clay 4, plus 0.5–2% chrome oxide or potassium dioxide (a soluble form of chrome), firing to around 900°C–950°C (1652°F–1742°F) to give red. Because of the low alumina content, the glaze may only be safely fired on flat surfaces or used with caution vertically. Increases in temperature encourage orange and yellow rather than red shades. A suggested recipe for 1080°C–1120°C (1976°F–2048°F) is lead monosilicate 55, whiting 10, feldspar 25, China clay 10 plus chrome oxide 2%.

**Nickel** Nickel oxide (NiO), a dark green or black powder, produces muddy greens and browns in most glazes but in suitable mixtures it will give creamy yellows, electric blues and vivid pinks. Like many other oxides used in small quantities, nickel is useful for softening colours of other oxides. It is excellent, for example, when used with cobalt for producing subtle shades of blue, violet and purple. But its most dramatic colours come in glazes containing zinc and barium when 1–3% nickel will give brilliant blues and pinks at stoneware temperatures. Such colours may be further modified by the addition of other oxides such as manganese to subdue the colour.

In glazes containing titanium dioxide small percentages of nickel will result in pale lemon yellows. The titanium forms an opaque glaze which is stained by the nickel. Nickel is not affected by the atmosphere of the kiln.

**Vanadium** Vanadium pentoxide ($V_2O_5$), a dark yellow powder, yields soft yellow and creams which can be strengthened in conjunction with titanium and tin oxide. In some glazes vanadium will give a pale blue. Because it is expensive and difficult to handle, at earthenware temperatures a yellow vanadium-tin commercial stain is used. At higher temperatures vanadium can result in mottled and broken cream-browns, but in amounts greater than 5% it can make the glaze dry and unpleasant. There is still much to find out about this oxide.

**Tin** Tin oxide, or stannic oxide, ($SnO_2$) is a fine white powder added to glazes at all temperatures to produce a smooth, milky opaque white. For hundreds of years tin oxide has been used as an excellent opacifier,

giving attractive whites when added in amounts from 6–15%, depending on the basic glaze. The white majolica glazes of the Italian renaissance and Dutch Delftware are some of the tin glazes which have made use of this material.

Some 2% of tin will go into solution in the glaze, larger amounts suspending themselves in the glaze matrix. Quantities around 6% can produce soft, semi-opaque effects which encourage iron specking in the glaze. The attraction of tin oxide, despite its cost, is the milky white quality of the results which cannot be equalled by any other material. In reduction tin can be greyed by the atmosphere, particularly in lead glazes at earthenware temperatures.

**Zircon** Zirconium oxide ($ZrO_2$), or zircon, zirconium silicate ($ZrO_2.SiO_2$), is used to opacify glazes to give a smooth creamy white surface. Zircon is refractory and can be used at any temperatures and fired in any atmosphere. Its use in glazes intended for functional purposes is thought to be advantageous because it has a hardening effect on the surface, making it more resistant to scratching. Weight for weight, the oxide form contains more zircon, but the silicate disperses better in the glaze though is about half as strong. A less effective opacifier than tin oxide weight for weight, up to 15–20% being needed to produce full opacity, it is often used as an alternative because it is a fraction of the price. In contrast to the milky blue characteristic of tin oxide, zirconium

gives a creamy white. Combinations of tin oxide and zirconium oxide can make use of the best qualities of each oxide.

**Titania** Titanium dioxide ($TiO_2$) is a white powder which causes opacity and mattness by creating a fine network of crystals in the structure of the glaze in amounts of 5–10%. Because of the crystal structure, titania can have a softening effect on oxides added to the glaze. In small quantities, titania makes iron oxide reddish-orange. At higher temperatures smaller amounts of titania (2–4%) can result in soft bluish or creamy shades.

# GLAZE STAINS

Commercially produced glaze stains (similar to body stains and underglaze and in-glaze colour), are made by heating metal oxides with other materials until fusion takes place and a chemical bond established. The resulting blocks of colour are then broken up, finely ground and washed. Commercial glaze stains suspend themselves in the glaze matrix and hence need to be regarded as opacifiers as well as colouring materials. Glaze stains considerably extend the range of colours available, but unlike most colouring metal oxides only very small amounts go into solution in the glaze giving opaque surfaces which can lack depth.

As ceramic technology has become more sophisticated, the colours available have increased, particularly at higher temperatures.

Red, a colour only previously possible at earthenware temperatures, is now reliably obtainable at stoneware temperatures.

Like any colouring material the result of adding stains depends on the glaze, as clear or semi-clear glazes will act differently to matt opaque glazes. Equally important is the amount of stain used in the glaze. Small quantities can give subtle colours, while larger amounts, though intensifying the colour, can look flat and lack visual interest. Despite the range of blues and greens offered, most produce similar results, particularly at higher temperatures. Different shades can be judiciously blended while stains can also be used with small quantities of colouring oxides.

Some stains benefit from wet grinding to further break down particle size, either in a pestle and mortar or ball mill. This reduces any tendency for specking of the colour though if the stains are ground too finely they cease to be effective. Potters can prepare their own stains but the process is lengthy and, in view of the commercial range available, may be considered unnecessary. Specialist books listed in Further Reading (page 94) give recipes for different colours.

27 **Sandy Brown** – *thrown and turned stoneware stemmed bowl with painted decoration using underglaze colours, about 35 cm (14 in.) tall, 1989. Bright, freely painted and trailed decoration adds colour and life to this special piece*

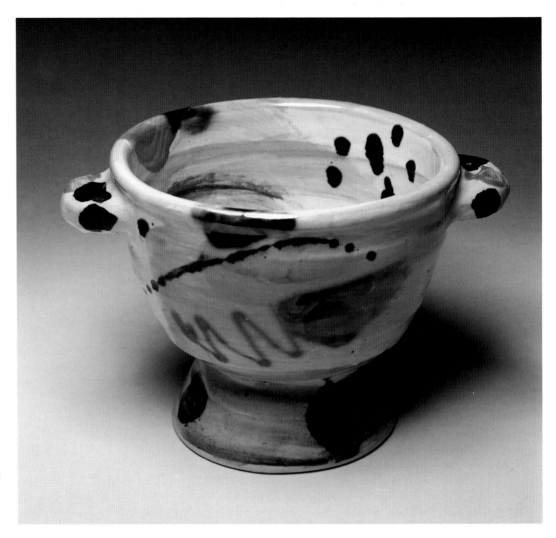

# CHAPTER FOUR

# APPLYING THE GLAZE

Discovering how glaze works not only involves finding out what it is made of, but also how it can be applied to exploit its full potential. Even at its simplest, a thin layer will give a different result to a thick application of most glazes. Such basic knowledge will enable the best results to be obtained.

Glaze is usually prepared in slop form as a smooth homogeneous mixture usually applied in the consistency of single cream, depending on the method of application. Glaze thickness, known as *specific gravity* (SG), can be accurately measured and checked against a known requirement by comparing the weight of a pint of prepared glaze slop with the correct measure. Water is a fixed constant 20oz to the pint (UK measure) and the thicker the mixture the heavier the same measure of glaze will weigh. Glaze intended for use on a porous surface needs to be about 31 fluid oz to the pint, while a thicker mixture of 34 fluid oz to the pint is required for vitrified surfaces.[1] Pint weight can literally be weighed or tested with a hydrometer, such as that used to measure the SG of car batteries, and purchased cheaply in a car accessory shop.

A simple homemade version of a hydrometer consists of a length of wood with a weight of some sort at one end. When lowered into a well-stirred glaze at the correct thickness it will always float at this depth. A mark on the wood at the point it lies in the glaze serves as a guide for future reference. If the mark is well above the glaze level the density is too high and more water is needed; if it sinks below the surface the density is too low and water needs to be removed. With experience, the glaze thickness will quickly be assessed by feel. Incidentally, the Imperial (British) pint measure given here should not be confused with the US measure which is of greater quantity:

1 Imperial pint = 1.205 US pints.
1 US pint      = 0.83 Imperial pints.

Glaze materials, suspended in the slop, settle over time and need thorough mixing before use. Settled glaze can most effectively be mixed by the hand which can feel if the ingredients are well distributed and can reach in the corners of the tub. This poses no problems for studio potters who tend to use only bucket-sized amounts of glaze. Only put one hand in the glaze slop at a time leaving the other clean and free for any emergencies. For potters who cannot or do not want to stir by hand electrical mixers can be equally effective. A kitchen sieve whisked round the stirred glaze will further help to break down any lumps. Glazes high in plastic ingredients need considerable stirring before a thorough mix is achieved. After use the inside surface of the glaze tub should be wiped clean with a rubber kidney or sponge to prevent drops of glaze drying and subsequently falling into the slop so making sieving necessary. Lids on buckets will protect the contents from drying out and keep out foreign bodies. All glaze containers should be clearly labelled.

[1]*Metric conversion*
1 oz = 28.35 gm
1 pt = 0.5683 litre
for UK pint weight to litre multiply by 0.5683
UK flu oz to cc multiply by 28.412
20 flu oz to the pint = 999.7 gm/litre
31 flu oz to the pint = 1546.5 gm/litre
34 flu oz to the pint = 1696.1 gm/litre

Glazes settle at different rates of time, some more rapidly than others. Those high in non-plastic ingredients settle quickly, the contents forming a layer, hard to dislodge, at the bottom of the bucket. Glazes high in plastic materials, such as clay, stay in suspension for longer periods and do not settle in such hard sediments. For this reason it is important when planning the make up of a glaze to incorporate clay if possible. Glazes which require a low alumina content can usefully incorporate a small amount of bentonite, a highly plastic form of clay roughly 12 times as plastic, weight for weight, as ball clay, 2% of which can be effective in aiding suspension without unduly influencing the appearance of the fired glaze. This small amount of clay can be made more effective by flocculating it with the addition of vinegar in the glaze slop. Larger additions of 6–8% bentonite can give glazes highly fluid handling qualities enabling them to be applied by painting. Because bentonite is so plastic, it can easily form soft lumps when added to the glaze which may even pass through the sieve and re-form on the other side. This problem can be avoided by mixing it with the other dry glaze ingredients or by soaking it in hot water over night before adding it to the glaze.

Commercial glaze suspenders such as synthetic gum, known as *CMC* or *Macaloid* are highly effective and only very small quantities are needed to ensure the glaze stays in suspension. Unlike organic alternatives, such as seaweed or gum arabic, such suspenders do not decay in the glaze and maintain their power over long periods of time.

As a practical aid to keeping glazes usable it is good practice to stir them once a week adding water if necessary; a ritual which avoids the settling problem and is seen as a part of regular studio maintenance.

Glaze materials, whether minerals, oxides or ready prepared glazes, are usually supplied in paper or plastic bags, and though clearly labelled when they arrive, over time may lose such vital information. Plastic and paper bags are almost impossible to maintain free of dust and in the dry heat of the pottery workshop deteriorate quickly. Ideally all glaze materials should be transferred to lidded plastic containers. These do not trap dust and can be regularly wet wiped clean. A label firmly tied (rather than glued) on the outside, or written with a waterproof felt-tipped pen, will serve as easy reference. A further label placed inside the container will help eliminate the problem of unidentified materials. Testing materials as described in chapter 1 indicates how differently they behave when fired and how similar they look in their pre-fired state. Test each new batch of material on a circular tile of about 5 cm (2 in) diameter marked on the reverse with its name and the supplier from whom it was obtained. Stored on the inside, the button will be a visual and practical record of the contents.

Mixing glaze, whether from a recipe or in prepared form, is relatively straightforward provided all the necessary scales and containers are to hand and are sufficiently large to hold the materials required. Ingredients need to be carefully weighed, preferably on scales with a pan able to hold the required amount. Sandwich plastic and non-plastic ingredients and, to avoid raising dust, add them gently to an excess of water. Hot water will speed up the slaking process (and in cold weather make mixing glaze far less painful), and the correct amount of water will enable the glaze to be used immediately. Leave to slake, which may take an hour or so, and once thoroughly wetted stir then sieve the slop through an 80s then a 120s mesh sieve. A stiff bristled brush, such as that used for washing-up, will aid the slop through the sieve.

The higher the number of the mesh, the finer are the holes, and the use of plenty of water makes this task much less troublesome. Two sets of sieves, one for white and one for coloured glazes will help prevent contamination, particularly of cobalt. Most materials are supplied dry having been finely ground and passed through a 300s mesh sieve and only require passing through an 80s mesh to produce a smooth homogeneous slop, but finer sievings do ensure a more thorough mix. The only materials regularly supplied damp (usually with 5–10% moisture) are flint and quartz to prevent them giving off dust, an aspect which needs to be taken into account when weighing out glaze. Over time this moisture will dry out and care has to be taken when handling these materials to avoid raising dust. If plenty of water has been used to mix the glaze, time will be needed for it to settle before water can be removed.

An alternative to sieving is to ball mill the glaze if suitable equipment is available. The charge should consist of roughly $\frac{1}{3}$ balls and $\frac{1}{3}$ glaze slop milled for two to three hours. Milling not only ensures a thorough mixing of all the ingredients but also grinds them to a finer particle size. This is especially useful for glazes containing raw minerals as they enter into fusion at a lower temperature without loss of quality and mature the glaze 10–20° below the usual point. A longer period of milling may be required if finer particle size is needed.

# GLAZE APPLICATION

Applying glaze may take as long as making the piece and requires careful preparation. Far from being a minor part of potting, glazing is as vital to the success of the pot as any making process.

Each method of glaze application has its own advantages, depending on the size of the piece and the effect required. All those described here are intended for biscuit fired porous pots which will quickly absorb glaze. A later section deals with applying glaze to pots which have been vitrified or have not been biscuit fired.

**Dipping** is the simplest method of applying glaze. A sufficiently large vat of glaze is needed into which the pot, held firmly by one hand, can be completely immersed or be dipped on the outside only. Where an all-over even coating of glaze is required dipping is efficient and quick, and once practice has been acquired gives smooth results. Pots have to be of a handleable size so control is maintained; large pots are heavy when full of glaze and difficult to manipulate. Pots suitable for dipping need walls sufficiently thick to allow them to absorb a coating of glaze without becoming saturated. Thin walls quickly become too wet to hold glaze which may run off the surface and, when dry, may develop hairline cracks and crawl during the firing.

To dip the pot hold it firmly, one finger on the rim and another on the base, gently plunge it into the well-stirred glaze, agitate for a second or two and lift out, allowing the glaze to pour from the inside. Wriggle the pot round to help runs smooth out. Within a few seconds the glaze should be absorbed and lose its shine. Until this happens the wet surface should not be touched as it will scar easily, though the base can be wiped clean with a finger or a rubber kidney before it is stood on a clean surface.

As the pot dries it is fettled, that is, made ready for the kiln. This involves cleaning the base with a sponge to remove any remaining glaze leaving a neat edge about 3 mm ($\frac{1}{8}$ in.) from the bottom. The exact distance depends on the viscosity of the glaze; those with a tendency to run may require a wider area to catch any glaze and prevent it flowing onto the kiln shelf. A resist painted on the base before glazing will leave a neat edge. Hot wax or commercially prepared water-based media are excellent. Resist applied to surfaces fired in contact with each other, such as lids and galleries, not only creates a neat, clean line but makes fettling easier. The proportion between unglazed and glazed areas can be crucial in determining the aesthetic appearance of the pot. Terracotta and reduction fired stoneware are attractive without glaze, but white earthenware and stoneware fired in the electric kiln have little intrinsic interest and are better glazed.

Bald patches caused by finger-marks can be dabbed with glaze using a glaze mop or a Chinese brush which carries a good quantity of glaze. Touching up such bald or thin patches is most safely carried out while the pot is slightly damp as it helps prevent blistering or blebbing which can occur when a wet glaze is put on top of a dry one. Finally, when the glaze is dry check for any undue runs or drips. These can be gently rubbed down with a finger or a wooden tool, taking great care to avoid removing too much thus leaving bald areas.

There are no specific rules about the thickness of glaze application as each is different, nor is it easy to test accurately the thickness that has been put on. Using the glaze at the correct thickness will help avoid this problem. Thickness can be tested with a sharp point of a pin or similar instrument. As a rough guide the glaze layer needs to be about 2 mm ($\frac{1}{12}$ in.) thick. Only experience in terms of the fired glaze will determine what thickness is needed and notes recording such information will prove invaluable for future reference.

**Pouring** Pouring glaze is useful for large pieces which cannot be easily manipulated, or where there is insufficient glaze to allow total immersion. First glaze the inside by pouring and swilling, working as quickly as possible to obtain an even covering. Glaze drops or dribbles on the outside should be scraped off and wiped clean with a sponge, and the pot left to dry before the outside is glazed. Depending on the size and weight of the pot, the outside can be held by the foot over a wide bowl and jugsful of glaze tipped down the outside. Larger pots may need to be rested on triangular supports across a bowl or other containers sitting on a banding wheel and the glaze poured on the outside while the whole is slowly revolved. Allow the glaze to lose its shine before touching it.

Some pots are best glazed by a combination of pouring and dipping. Once the inside has been glazed by pouring and swilling and allowed to dry, the outside can

*28* **Richard Slee** – Three Flasks, *slip cast, earthenware, 20 cm (8 in.) tall, 1989. The organic form of these strong bottles is sensitively revealed by the subtle effects of colour sprayed on the transparent glaze*

be covered by holding the pot upside down by the foot and gently lowering it in the glaze. Holding the pot perfectly level will ensure air is trapped inside. Should any air escape, then its place will be taken by glaze. Dipping in this way can produce an even coating of glaze.

**Spraying** Spraying produces carefully controlled even surfaces; its major disadvantage is the need for complex and efficient spray and extraction equipment. The fine spray of glaze made up of airborne particles must not be inhaled, neither must it be allowed to float around the workshop where it can settle and be disturbed on future occasions so posing a long term threat to health. Full and adequate precautions must be taken to prevent this happening. Spraying has many advantages. Glaze can be applied in thin coats without pours or drips, or it can be graduated so different thickness can be obtained. Further advantages are that only small quantities of glaze are required and one glaze can be sprayed over another for decorative effect.

Basic equipment includes a *compressor*, a *spray booth* fitted with a turntable and a sufficiently powerful *extraction fan* to vent the glaze spray to a safe exit or through a suitable system of filters. Excellent commercial equipment, usually intended for industrial use, is available but tends to be expensive. Homemade equipment should not compromise on safety given the need to avoid inhaling the glaze spray. Glaze to be sprayed

needs to be finely ground and put through a fine sieve of at least 120s mesh to prevent the nozzle of the spray gun clogging up.

Pots with narrow necks should first be swilled out with glaze and allowed to dry before spraying the outside. On open pots such as bowls, the inside is sprayed first and allowed to dry before being stood upside down on a central support and the outside glazed. Hold the spray nozzle about 30–45 cm (12–18 in.) from the pot while slowly revolving it on the turntable. If sprayed too

29  **Andrew McGarva** – *thrown and turned reduction-fired stoneware mugs with painted oxide decoration over the glaze, 1987. A skilled decorator, Andrew McGarva has related the figurative decoration to the simple but attractive shapes*

close wet patches will result giving an uneven surface, if too far away too much glaze is lost. As the pot turns, so layers of glaze are formed and an even covering obtained. Sprayed glaze can look rough and uneven and may appear thicker or thinner than is required. The texture built up by spraying will smooth out during the firing on well melted glazes and pose no problem. On matt, stiff glazes the texture may not smooth over entirely and this can be incorporated as a decorative element, or a different system can be used for the glaze application.

Pots which have been taken to a high temperature and are vitrified can safely be sprayed if they are first heated up gently until they are about 160°C (320°F). At this point they are too hot to touch and must be picked up with a cloth or tongs. The heat causes the glaze to dry quickly and stay on the surface.
**Painting** Glaze mixed with a suitable binder can be successfully painted on biscuit or unfired pots (known as *green ware*) to form a non-powdery layer. Painting glaze gives greater control against overlaps or runs. Once each layer has dried further coats either of the same or another glaze can be applied. Unfired pots must be treated with care and lifted up with both hands, never by the rim. Apply the glaze in thin layers to prevent the walls becoming soaked with water causing them to collapse.

*30* **Emmanuel Cooper** *– jug form, thrown and assembled, high-fired porcelain, clear glaze containing a small amount of tin oxide over painted cobalt and chrome decoration, 25 cm (10 in.) tall, 1990. The freely painted decoration animates the modelled form of the jug to good effect*

The most common binding agent is gum arabic. It is cheap and efficient and if bought as a powder can quickly be dissolved in water; the crystals need to be soaked for a day or two before they will dissolve. The gum arabic solution replaces some of the liquid in the glaze and so water has to be removed while the glaze is settled or it will be too thin. Such a glaze is much thicker than normal and is applied with a broad, soft, household paint brush. When the first coat is dry a further coat, or coats, will increase the thickness of the application and help achieve a smooth layer. Gum arabic, an organic material, starts to decay after several days giving off a strong sour smell, but its qualities remain unaffected. During the firing gum arabic burns away giving off a pungent odour like bad fish. Alternatives to gum arabic (which can be purchased as a white commercially marketed paper glue) are bentonite and a commercial glaze suspender such as CMC.

Glaze loaded with a binder such as gum arabic or CMC can be successfully painted on vitrified surfaces. It is also a satisfactory way of re-glazing fired pots, particularly if they have been warmed up first, and is a useful method of saving pots which have not been correctly glazed.

Many ceramic suppliers now offer a range of ready prepared brush-on glazes. These tend to give special effects which offer unique decorative qualities such as gold speckles or snowflake texture. Brush-on glazes are supplied in liquid form in small containers

and manufacturers give clear instructions for their use. They need thorough stirring to ensure the ingredients are well mixed and if too thick can be thinned with a little water or medium sold by the supplier. Adjusting such prepared glazes is virtually impossible as their ingredients are not disclosed. While brush-on glazes are expensive, they offer a further range to the studio potter's palette with highly professional effects.

*31  Seth Cardew – dish, stoneware, thrown and turned with iron painted decoration, reduction fired, 28 cm (11 in.), 1987. The well-placed decoration makes effective use of the form of the dish*

# CHAPTER FIVE

# DECORATING WITH GLAZE

The previous chapter described how to apply glaze to achieve as even and controlled a layer as possible, avoiding runs and overlaps which can mar the overall effect. This chapter deals with developing the qualities of glaze and how it can be decorated with a wide range of techniques.

The simplest method of decorating is to make use of single and double thicknesses. A pot dipped and then partly dipped (or poured) again can produce attractive contrasts. The glaze has to lose its shine before a further coat is applied but it must not become too dry or the first layer may blister and bleb. If a second layer is applied while the first is still shiny it may not take this and the first may be washed off. For double glazing, whether dipping or pouring, the time gap is crucial for successful results.

Pouring glaze can be an equally attractive method of achieving simple but lively

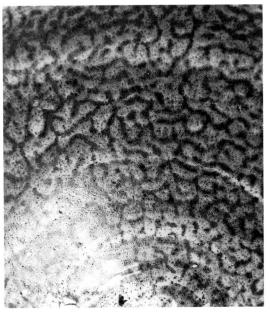

*32* **Peter Beard** – *slab built stoneware vase form with slip and glaze decoration, about 30 cm (12 in.) tall, 1990. A successful use of textured glaze over a reactive slip*

*33 A white stoneware glaze with 6% tin oxide applied over a vitreous slip containing 50% red iron oxide which breaks through the glaze to give the mottled effect*

surfaces. Aprons of glaze poured down the sides of a pot either at random or in sequence, can quickly enliven and animate a surface.

## DECORATIVE SLIPS

Poured or dipped glaze can be particularly effective if used in conjunction with clay slips applied to the surface of the pot which react with the glaze. Slips can be made up of a light or white firing clay which may be coloured by the addition of metal oxide or prepared body stain. A white firing ball clay will often function as a base for bright coloured slips while dark firing clays can be used for darker shades. Both may need adjusting to fit the body as slip and body must contract at the same rate to ensure a tight fit. Up to 40% China clay can be incorporated to whiten slips and reduce shrinkage. Slips are usually applied to leatherhard clay though some are slipped when bone dry. Slip the inside by swilling and pouring and allow this to become leatherhard or dry before covering

the outside by dipping or pouring. This
avoids over-wetting which may cause blisters
in the body as air is trapped, or collapsing it
by making it too soft.

Slips serve as a buffer between glaze and
body, preventing interaction. White slips help
to brighten glaze while the addition of oxides
can add colour and texture. Slips containing
oxides develop their colour when 'wetted' by
glaze; transparent glazes give the brightest
colours; while opaque glazes, though
attractive because of their lack of reflection,
tend to obscure it. Slip overloaded with oxide
can react with the glaze, flooding it with
colour and textures breaking the surface.
Slips loaded with such materials as silica,
alumina or silicon carbide can yield a range
of visual effects. Silicon carbide reacts with
the glaze causing local reduction, converting
oxides such as copper from green to red, and
also releasing gases which in well-melted
glazes escape but in matt glazes can be
trapped resulting in attractive volcanic
surfaces with no sharp edges. Stiff matt glazes
high in barium carbonate seem to give the
best results over white slips bearing up to 3%
silicon carbide.

Slips loaded with fluxes such as whiting or

*34  **Emmanuel Cooper** – Hot Summer, jug,
thrown and modelled porcelain with slip
under tin glaze, 20 cm (8 in.) tall, 1991. The
matt white glaze over a slip gives a rich
textured glaze which is both smooth and well
controlled*

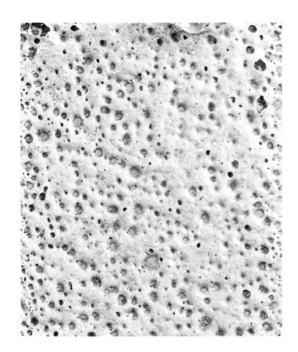

35   *Volcanic glaze with silicon carbide giving a smooth bubbled surface, stoneware.* RECIPE: *borax frit 45, zinc oxide 18, China clay 15, flint 15, feldspar 7 + rutile 6% and silicon carbide (fine) 4%*

36   **Emmanuel Cooper** *– thrown and turned lidded porcelain jar, 18 cm (7 in.) tall, 1985. The spiral decoration was created by throwing two bodies together, one of which had 2% copper carbonate wedged into it. The high soda glaze crazes over the copper*

zinc oxide work in a different way, but can give attractive glazes. Success depends on the glaze composition and the thickness of application. Matt glazes tend to block reactions while clear, satin matt or transparent mixtures may give livelier results.

# GLAZE ON GLAZE

Like slip, glaze can be trailed either directly on the surface of the clay or, more usually, on a layer of glaze. Because glaze does not have the fluid, smooth qualities of slip it may need to be modified by the addition of bentonite.

Janice Tchalenko and Clive Davies are two potters who have developed this technique to perfection. Both use a white glaze as a base which takes up and reflects the colours of the trailed decoration to spectacular effect. Experience is needed to find the correct consistency; if too thin it will run and lose definition, if too thick it will not flow, or it will leave too wide a line. Suitable trailing tools include rubber syringes and recycled plastic bottles fitted with nozzles. The size of the hole in the nozzle will determine the thickness of the glaze trail and experiments will be needed to establish how this can most effectively be done.

In addition to trailing, glaze can be applied by stamps, sponges, painting and sprays. Stamps can be cut out of fine foam, loaded with glaze and pressed on the glaze. The secret is to ensure the correct amount of glaze is taken up and the foam reloaded each time to obtain even results. Several different glazes applied in this way give rich and colourful patterns. Glaze reacts with the body during firing and the layer has to be sufficiently thick not to be 'eaten away' which can result in a thin, washed out effect.

Though foam stamps can have a mechanical appearance, the variations in glaze load will give the decoration its own unique qualities, with the slight unevenness of the colour thickness adding visual interest. Sponges work in much the same way but with more random patterning. Applying glaze by painting presents more problems in that the brush can lift off as well as deposit glaze. Decoration has to be thought of in ceramic rather than watercolour terms, with designs made up of single strokes rather than large washes. Once applied, it is difficult to touch up the design without spoiling the crispness of the stroke.

Spraying glaze, discussed at length in the previous chapter, can be used for air-brush designs. Small areas sprayed with a mouth diffuser, such as those used by commercial artists to blow on colour, can be effective. Alternatively, glaze can be flicked from short stiff bristles, such as those on a toothbrush, giving speckles and spots to the glaze. To avoid blotches, the brush needs to be charged each time with a minimum of glaze. Flicking or blowing glaze through a diffuser does not present the same health and safety problems as spraying with a compressor as the particles

*37 (Right)* **Janice Tchalenko** *– thrown and turned stoneware bowl, reduction fired with glaze on glaze decoration, about 35 cm (14 in.) across, 1989. One glaze trailed over another gives this vibrant decorative effect*

*38* **Janice Tchalenko** *– thrown and turned stoneware teapot with glaze over glaze decoration, reduction fired, 15 cm (6 in.) tall, 1985. The lively throwing and perky spout make this a decorative as well as a functional teapot*

*39 (Above)* **Kate Malone** – *double sided bowl, carved bowl, white earthenware with multi-coloured glaze, about 13 cm (5 in.) tall, 1990. By adding colouring metal oxides and glaze stains to a basic commercially produced glaze, a highly textured glaze surface is produced*

*40 (Left)* **Kate Malone** – *double vessel form, press-moulded and handbuilt, earthenware, about 23 cm (9 in.) tall, 1990. This ingenious vessel calls on the rich tradition of art pottery to create the fantastic shape, while the richly textured surface is made up from a commercial transparent glaze to which various oxides have been added*

*41 (Right)* **Clive Davies** – *stoneware bowl, wheel thrown with applied glaze decoration, reduction fired, 28 cm (11 in.) diameter, 1990. Glaze applied over glaze produced this rich effect which recalls the Impressionists' technique*

are fewer in number and larger in size, but care has to be taken to ensure no glaze gets in the mouth. Nevertheless, the processes are best carried out in the open, rather than indoors, so that air-borne particles are quickly dispersed.

# PIGMENT DECORATION

The use of commercially produced stains and oxides for colouring glaze is discussed in Chapter 3, but colour can also be applied under or on top of a glaze. Low temperature glaze, known as *enamel*, is applied on a fired glaze and fixed in a third low-temperature firing.

Underglaze decoration, either in the form of colouring oxides or commercially produced underglaze stains, is applied on biscuit-fired pots under a clear or semi-clear glaze. During the firing the colour is taken into the glaze, when a certain amount of blurring occurs. Such pigments can be applied by any of the methods described earlier – spraying, stamping, painting and so on – the most usual being painting. Pigments vary in strength and the amount needed to give a

42 **Sandy Brown** – Can You Can Can *dish, press-moulded with many coloured glazes applied, stoneware, 38 cm (15 in.) across, 1991. The vigorous decoration with its freely interpreted figure is sensitively carried out and well suited to the shape of the dish*

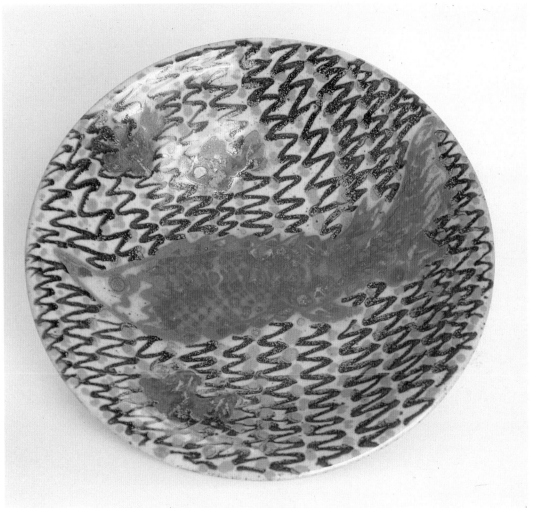

43  **Bernard Leach** – Bird Plate, *thrown and turned reduction fired stoneware with resist decoration, c 1950. Wax decoration painted over the dark tenmoku glaze has been overpainted with iron to give the rich subtle effect*

44  **Janice Tchalenko** – *dish, thrown and turned stoneware with glaze trailed decoration on base white glaze, reduction fired, 30 cm (12 in.) diameter, 1980. The fish set against the net decoration has an attractive fluid quality*

good colour without saturating the glaze varies from stain to stain. Classic examples of underglaze painting are the blue and white porcelains of the Chinese Ming dynasty which make full use of the contrast between the blue-grey of the cobalt pigment and the intense white of the body. Successful designs achieve a balance between background and painted decoration.

Underglaze colours vary according to the firing temperature – the lower the temperature the greater the number of colours available. Metal oxides mixed with a little water and ground with a palette knife will give the range of colours described in detail in Chapter 3, depending on the make up of the glaze. Thickly applied pigment may cause the covering glaze to crawl as the powder acts like a layer of tiny ball-bearings. Mixing the pigment with a little glaze or some other medium, such as gum arabic, will help bind it and prevent the problem.

Commercially produced underglaze colours

45 **Glenys Barton** – Profile Head I, *modelled stoneware head, about 38 cm (15 in.) tall, 1986. The textured glaze adds an extra dimension to this powerfully conceived head.* Photograph by Karen Norquay

46 **Angus Suttie** – Jug Form, *handbuilt, high fired earthenware with slip and oxide decoration, about 51 cm (20 in.) tall, 1989. The painted decoration is an integral part of the fascination of the handbuilt form*

offer a wide palette and have the advantage of staying the same as, or very similar to, their unfired colour. All colours will fire to earthenware temperatures, a few will fire successfully to stoneware. Like oxides, stains are mixed with a little water or a medium, such as gum arabic (suppliers often market a suitable medium), and ground on a glass sheet. Because underglaze colours, such as metal oxides, are taken in the glaze, pattern and decoration may lose definition, becoming slightly blurred. Mixing the colour with a little clay will help stabilize it.

**In-glaze** is the name given to coloured pigments painted on top of the glaze before it is fired. During firing the colour sinks into the glaze, hence its name. The most well known historical example is majolica, tin-glazed earthenware decorated with a range of designs and colours painted on the white glaze which includes Delftware, Italian majolica and Spanish Hispano-Moresque wares.

Though traditionally associated with tin-glazed earthenware and a wide palette, in-glaze decoration can successfully be developed on stonewares and on a range of

**47  Jill Fanshawe Kato** – Pheasant Plate, *dish with tropical motif in black, green, blue, orange, beige and grey, stoneware, handbuilt, 45 cm (18 in.) across, c 1989. The combination of the lively form with the well-placed paper-resist decoration has resulted in a pleasing pot using a semi-matt glaze*

**48  Joanna Howells** – *dish, bottle and jug, thrown and turned stoneware with painted decoration, dish about 23 cm (9 in.) across, c 1989. Altogether an attractive and imaginative use of simple form and well conceived decoration*

glazes. Iron pigments applied on an unfired glaze, for example, can develop rich rusty blacks and browns in the reduction atmosphere of the stoneware kiln. When incorporated with other oxides, such as cobalt, attractive effects can be obtained.

In-glaze colours can yield deep colours at both earthenware and stoneware temperatures. Whether oxides or stains, the pigment is best ground with a little water or recommended medium. Any of the methods of application described earlier are suitable but care has to be taken to avoid over-wetting the surface or blistering or lifting of the glaze may occur, a fault which is difficult to remedy. One method round this is to harden-on the glaze by firing it to biscuit temperature when it is fused but not fluxed. On raw glaze, splashes or accidents can either be gently scraped off or the entire layer washed off and, when dry, re-glazed.

**On-glaze**  On-glaze, or enamel, is applied on the fired glaze and consists of low temperature glazes which melt and fuse around 750°C–800°C (1382°F–1482°F). Enamels can be purchased as ready prepared powders from suppliers who offer a wide range of colours in carefully worked out glaze

bases. Like all ceramic glazes enamels are
made up of fluxes with alumina and silica
plus the colouring oxides. Lead is one of the
most useful fluxes at these low temperatures,
but boric oxide, sodium and potassium may
also be used. Enamels must be handled with
as much care as any other glazes to avoid
ingesting them in any way.

Enamels are ground with a medium, such
as fat or aniseed oil, to give a stiffish mixture
sufficiently fluid to be applied to the fired
glaze without losing definition. Water does
not bind the pigment satisfactorily. Before
applying enamel the surface of the pot has
first to be cleaned of dust and grease from the
fingers using methylated spirits. Painting is
the most popular method of application, but
any of the techniques described earlier can be
used. The art of enamel painting not only
depends on skilled application but on having
the pigment at the correct consistency.

For an even covering, known as *ground
laying*, enamel powder is gently dusted on a
surface on which a thin layer of fat oil has
been applied. One of the attractions of
enamel is the range and delicacy of colour
and the jewel-like effects which can be
obtained. The firing needs to be sufficiently

49　**John Maltby** – *detail from press-
moulded square dish, stoneware with slip and
enamel decoration, about 25 cm (10 in.),
1989. A highly successful combination of
form and painted decoration which celebrate
the subtle qualities of ceramics*

50   **Russell Coates** – *press-moulded white-glazed porcelain dish with Japanese type enamel decoration, 23 cm (9 in.) square, 1988*

51   **Paul Jackson** – *jug, red earthenware with painted decoration, thrown and turned, about 23 cm (9 in.) tall, c 1989. By dividing the upper part of the jug into panels the potter has been able to combine form and decoration in a lively composition all helped by the transparent glaze*

high for the glaze to soften allowing the enamel to sink in slightly. Suitable firing temperatures of enamel (and lustre) are not only determined by its make up but also by the softening temperature of the glaze – earthenware glazes soften at lower temperatures than stoneware or porcelain.

# GLASS AND LUSTRE DECORATION

*Lustre* and *glass pieces* are two other methods of decorating the surface of fired glaze. In the latter, pieces of glass are literally placed inside a bowl or on a flat surface over a light coloured glaze and fired in the kiln when the glass melts to form a pool of colour. Because of the different shrinkage between the body and the glass, the glass may craze badly but the effect can be colourful and decorative. The firing temperature depends on the type of glass, but the usual enamel temperature is a useful guide.

Lustre is the process in which a metal lustrous coating is put on the surface of a

52  **Anvil Pottery** – Wassail Bowl, *thrown and turned red earthenware with incised decoration through white slip, about 35 cm (14 in.) tall, c 1989. This modern interpretation of a traditional form is freely modelled with amusing modelled additions, the clear glaze bringing out decoration and form*

fired glaze. There are two sorts; one involves applying a mixture of metal salts and clay on a fired glaze and then firing to low temperature in a reduction atmosphere. The process is complex and the results elusive as the glaze has to be responsive to the metal vapour given off during reduction. This specialist technique is outside the scope of this book but these attractive effects are well worth investigating. Books dealing with this process are listed on page 94.

Lustres are also available as commercially prepared liquid resinates which are simply painted onto a fired glaze and re-fired to enamel temperature. They offer different effects to reduction lustres and are relatively simple to apply and fire. Colours range from brilliant gold, silver, ruby, copper to mother of pearl which can be highly effective when combined with dark or light coloured glazes. Subtle rather than bold effects tend to work best. Lustres are applied to the surface of the glaze and when fired to the appropriate temperature of 700°C–750°C (1292°F–1382°F), a thin metal layer is deposited. They can be applied by any of the techniques discussed earlier. Allow lustres, like enamels, to dry thoroughly before firing.

Enamels and prepared lustres can also be applied on fired glazes in the form of printed transfers or decals. This system involves the preparation of screens, special colours and so on. A full description of these techniques can be found in the books listed in Further Reading on page 94.

53  **Oriel Harwood** – Cornucopia, *press-moulded shape with dark copper lustre finish, 20 cm (8 in.) tall, 1988. The shell-like form is made almost surreal by the metallic-like finish*

# CHAPTER SIX

# KILNS AND FIRING

Successful glazes depend on successful firing. A wide range of relatively low priced and economical kilns are available. The introduction of highly efficient insulating materials has lowered the weight of kilns and reduced their overall size without loss of firing space, thus vastly increasing their efficiency and enabling both gas-fired and electric kilns to be portable. Kiln sizes range from 1 to over 20 cu ft (30–600 cu cm), but a useful average size electric kiln is about 3–6 cu ft (90–180 cu cm) firing chamber. This may be top or side loading and fitted with a variety of heat controls.

Electric, gas and oil kilns are all commercially available. With flame-burning kilns, the smaller the firing chamber the less efficient they tend to be. Potters firing with wood either construct their own or commission one from an experienced kiln builder. Sensitive but powerful burners have been developed for flame-burning kilns to enable them to operate efficiently with relatively small sized firing chambers. Unlike electric kilns, which if small need no special extraction system to remove gases and fumes

given off during the firing, flame-burning kilns are more complex and require a flue of some sort to duct away the burning gases. Flame-burning kilns cannot be safely used without such ventilation but many smaller kilns can be fired out of doors without a chimney. Before buying any kiln study the manufacturer's specifications and discuss with them your requirements. The experience of other potters is also well worth seeking.

Practical considerations such as the availability of single or three phase electrical power, the safe storage of gas cylinders or oil and adequate means of ventilation are all factors to take into account when choosing a kiln. The different effects of firing in electric and flame-burning kilns may also influence choice, the latter enabling a reduction atmosphere to be obtained.

Electric kilns are, basically, insulated boxes for retaining heat emitted by elements placed round the inside walls and floor. The atmosphere remains more or less unchanged though some local reduction may take place as organic materials burn away. The neutral or ordinary atmosphere in electric kilns

(sometimes called an oxidizing or neutral atmosphere) offers possibilities for bright colours and textural effects not obtainable in reduction firings where the flame can mar or obscure subtle shades while bringing out others. Biscuit firings, which need to be carried out slowly particularly in the early stages, are more easily carried out in electric kilns where temperature rise can be more easily controlled. Earthenware is usually fired in electric kilns.

Flame-burning kilns are mostly used for reduction fired stoneware and porcelain. During the firing the atmosphere in the kiln is starved of air by manipulating air inlets and outlets so creating a smoky atmosphere. Flames, hungry for oxygen, will attempt to take it from the glaze and the body. Iron relatively quickly releases its oxygen changing its colour; iron in the clay takes on a rich toasted hue while tiny specks enlarge to become spots which, if the reduction is very heavy, can bleed into the glaze. Copper is also affected by reduction, changing from its more common green state to pinks and deep reds. In well controlled flame-burning kilns the atmosphere can be easily manipulated, but in practice most have a slight reduction effect, which is an accepted part of their character.

Creating a reduction atmosphere in an electric kiln is more difficult. Few have the necessary flue to vent away fumes and the reduction causes the wire elements to burn away quickly, so shortening their life. Silicon carbide rod elements, fitted in some electric kilns, are unaffected by a reduction atmosphere. Such an atmosphere can be created by burning gas or organic materials, for example wood, in the firing chamber. Some form of extraction, such as a hood over the kiln with a powerful extractor fan, is required to vent the gases and fumes released out of the kiln room.

The choice of kilns, therefore, though governed by practical considerations, is also influenced by the effects offered by each type of firing. Size is an equally important consideration. Kilns need to be able to accommodate the size and quantity of the pots, but not so large that they deter experiment. Ideally potters need two kilns, one for carrying out tests, the other for firing finished work, though a satisfactory

54  **Richard Batterham** – *small tazza, thrown and turned stoneware, reduction fired with ash glaze, 15 cm (6 in.) tall, c 1989. This classic stemmed bowl, delicate fluted decoration and thinly applied ash glaze make a highly satisfying pot*

compromise has to be found. A final point to bear in mind is the level of future production.

Electric kilns should be installed by a suitable qualified electrician and located in a well ventilated space. During firings, gases and fumes are released by the clay and while acceptable in very low quantities they should not be inhaled in concentrated form. Large kilns need an extraction hood to vent off fumes and the kiln room should be well ventilated. An extractor fan fitted near the kiln will also help to remove fumes.

# HEAT CONTROL

Kilns have two main controls, one for the input of fuel into the kiln to enable the temperature to rise at the appropriate rate, the other to indicate the temperature inside the chamber. Electric kilns are fitted with a variety of switches; the simplest, with settings for low, medium and high, are turned manually. A more sophisticated system has a regulator which, according to the setting, turns the kiln on or off automatically. At a setting of 50, the power is on and off for the same length of time, usually about half a minute. More sophisticated programmes using mini-computers automatically conduct the firing to a pre-set schedule.

Flame-burning kilns are more complex. Gas and oil cannot be controlled as readily as electricity simply because limiting the fuel input and shortening the size of the flame

puts it at risk from being extinguished. Low settings may need close attention to ensure this does not happen. The early stages of firing are crucial as the temperature rise must be sufficiently slow to allow all moisture to escape without causing the pot to explode. Kilns fired by wood (or other solid fuel) enable the heat to be built up slowly over a period of time.

# TEMPERATURE INDICATORS

There are two main methods of indicating temperature inside the firing chamber; *pyrometric cones* or *bars* which soften and bend at a known temperature according to their composition, and a *pyrometer* which constantly shows internal temperature.

Cones are compounded from varying proportions of glaze materials and are marked with a number coded with the temperature at which they bend. 2.5–8 cm (1–3 in.) tall, triangular and pointed in shape, appropriate cones are placed in a stand or supported by a coil of clay and placed inside the chamber so that their reference number is visible through the spy hole. Usually three cones are used, one to serve as a signal immediately below the required point, one at the required temperature and one immediately above to indicate over-firing. In reduction kilns a cone is also used to signal when reduction should start. Cones are said

to have matured when they have bent over and 'touched their toes'.

Bars, like cones, are graded to soften at specific temperatures. They are some 50 mm (2 in.) in length and supported horizontally at each end in a refractory stand. When mature the bar sags in the centre. Bars are used in some kilns as a trigger to turn off the power and they are often employed in the ceramic industry to check firing temperature. All cones and bars need to be kept dry to ensure their abilities are not impaired.

Unlike more mechanical systems, pyrometric cones and bars indicate heat work carried out in the firing chamber. Like the ceramics being fired, they react to the effects of heat rather than ambient temperature. Their disadvantage is that they do not indicate the rise and fall of temperature which can only be done by a continuous system of measurement such as by a pyrometer.

Pyrometers rely on a highly sensitive measurement of metal expansion recorded as an electric current and indicated on a dial. They consist of a *thermocouple*, placed inside the kiln inside a protective porcelain sheath which is connected to an indicating dial more accurately called a *galvanometer*. Two different metal strips inside the thermocouple expand and contract according to temperature, giving off a slight electrical current which is indicated on the dial. Pyrometers have the great advantage of showing the temperature inside the kiln at all points of the firing thus allowing its rise and fall to be plotted. Digital indicators are particularly useful in reduction firings where a balance has to be struck between holding a smoky reducing atmosphere whilst at the same time maintaining and increasing temperature. Even subtle adjustments to the damper can affect this and changes will be instantly shown on the digital display.

A further useful temperature check is an automatic cut off to prevent over-firing. Once a suitable firing schedule has been evolved and the pack of the kiln made sufficiently uniform, firing devices can be highly accurate. Usual practice is to use both cones and pyrometer to ensure accuracy.

# FIRING PROCEDURES

As clay is fired it undergoes great physical and chemical changes, of which the major ones are discussed here as is their effect on the kiln firing. More detailed information can be found in the books listed on page 94.

One of the major effects of heat is to drive off water. In the first stage, known as the *smoking period*, physically combined water in the clay is driven off as steam. While most

55 **Richard Batterham** – *thrown and turned lidded pot, reduction-fired stoneware with white ash glaze, 22 cm (8½ in.) tall, 1989. The thinly applied ash glaze enhances the simplicity of this strong form*

water will dry out before the pot is fired, a certain amount remains. Temperature rise between room temperature, 20°C (68°F) and the boiling point of water, 100°C (212°F) needs to be very slow to allow steam to escape; too rapid a rise may cause steam to form too quickly and the consequent increase in volume (steam takes up more space than water) may cause the clay to shatter. The thicker the clay, the slower the temperature should rise. Pots which shatter are often thought to contain trapped air, but this is usually due to the presence of moisture.

The chemical formula of clay, $Al_2O_3.2SiO_2.2H_2O$, indicates that water, known as *the water of formation*, is combined in the crystal structure, and this gradually starts to be released around 350°C (662°F) continuing to around 600°C (1112°F). More steam is released in this process which changes the clay irreversibly into ceramic material. One other important change which starts at this point is the burning away of carbonaceous material given off as a pale blue smoke. Significant changes also occur to the crystalline structure of silica. As the temperature continues to rise the alumina and silica, prompted by the fluxes, gradually start to fuse into a glassy state.

In studio ceramics the first or biscuit firing is to 980°C–1000°C (1795°F–1832°F) at which point the body is porous but strong enough to be handled. Below this temperature most clays lack sufficient physical and mechanical strength as well as porosity.

# PREPARING FOR THE KILN

**Fettling**, the general term given to preparing work for the kiln, includes checking pots for any rough areas which can be smoothed over; for glazed pots the base or foot ring is cleaned, ensuring that a neat edge is left with sufficient bare body to prevent glaze running on the kiln shelf and touching up any bald patches left by finger marks. As different glazes look similar at this stage an identifying mark written with a soft pencil on the surface of the glaze can eliminate confusion and will burn away during the firing. A thin coating of alumina hydrate painted between surfaces which are to be fired together once the glaze has been wiped away (such as in the galleries of teapots and store jars) will prevent them sticking at stoneware temperature.

Kiln shelves should be kept clean and free of glaze spots. A carborundum stone rubbed over the shelf (**wear protective glasses to protect the eyes from flying splinters**) will remove drops of glaze or thin slivers of clay. **On no account** test for smoothness by rubbing your fingers over the surface; slivers of clay or daggers of glaze are razor sharp and can cut you badly. A thin coating of alumina hydrate painted or carefully dusted on the shelf will help stop pots sticking. Pots with glazes known to be susceptible to running can be stood on a thin pad of biscuit fired clay to protect the kiln shelf. If accidents

do occur, glaze may need to be chipped out of the shelf using a sharp chisel, with the shelf resting on a flat surface with a good padding under it such as a folded towel. Cones supported in clay should be allowed to dry thoroughly before being fired.

Kiln shelves are usually supported by three props. This eliminates rocking and reduces the amount of kiln furniture required. Any uneven shelves can be levelled up with pads of soft clay mixed with alumina hydrate, known as *wads*.

# BISCUIT FIRING

In the first, or *biscuit firing*, the ware is taken to the point at which the body is porous and absorbent but sufficiently strong to handle and glaze. The second, or *glaze firing*, is to a higher temperature. This contrasts with industrial production where the ware is first fired in a bisc or bisque to a point at which the body becomes hard and vitrified followed by a glaze (or glost) firing is to a lower temperature. It is much easier to apply glaze to absorbent biscuit than vitrified clay. During the glaze firing body and glaze react together.

Before packing the kiln check that it is in good working condition with no loose bits which could fall on the ware and, in electric kilns, check that all the elements are working. A vacuum cleaner will quickly remove all dust and bits of clay. Because unglazed pots do not stick together, biscuit firings can be packed tightly, allowing room for the expansion and contraction of the clay as it heats and cools during the firing. Pots can be stacked rim to rim so long as the weight is evenly distributed. If cones are to be used these should be placed in the kiln and their position checked by shining an electric torch through the spy hole or placing a lighted candle inside the kiln which is removed before firing.

The initial temperature rise should be slow, no more than 30°C (104°F) an hour to allow water to be driven off. All dampers should be open for steam to escape. Once 150°C–200°C (294°F–392°F) has been reached the firing can be speeded up, any vent closed with maximum input reached around 500°C (932°F). A dull red heat starts around 550°C–600°C (1022°F–1112°F) which gets brighter as the temperature continues until by 980°C (1795°F) a good red glow is evident. Top temperature in a 3–6 cubic foot kiln may take 8–12 hours depending on the thickness of the ware, thinner walled pieces can be fired more quickly. Some clays require a 'soak' at 900°C (1652°F) for an hour when the temperature is held to allow any carbon in the body to burn away completely. This helps prevent bloating of the body when it is subsequently fired to higher temperatures. When top temperature is reached leave the kiln to cool to 200°C (392°F) before opening the vent and 100°C–150°C (212°F–302°F) before opening the door.

56   *Bloating in the body which occurred during the stoneware glaze firing either because the body was taken to too high a temperature or because the carbon in the clay had not been allowed to burn away fully during the biscuit firing*

# GLAZE FIRING

After glazing allow the pots to become thoroughly dry before packing the kiln. Unlike biscuit, pots with glaze need to sit directly on clean and even kiln shelves, packed to make as economical use of the space as possible. First, sort out ware of similar height and plan accordingly. Biscuit fired pots can be fired more quickly, but it is cautious to start with gentle heat speeding up more quickly to higher temperatures.

A short soak of 15 to 30 minutes at top temperature will ensure fully matured glazes both for earthenware and stoneware, but at the higher temperatures the firing tends to be slower and this allows time for maturation. In practice the slower the firing the richer and more interesting the glaze. Fast fired wares often lack the depth and quality of slower fired pieces.

Colour in the kiln changes as the temperature rises. At 1100°C (2012°F) a red-orange can be seen, becoming bright orange at 1200°C (2192°F). Beyond this point it is advisable to peer in the kiln only with the aid of a transparent sheet of dark blue glass which protects the eyes from heat, glare and infra-red light. At 1260°C (2300°F) the colour is a bright yellow. Once top temperature is reached a short soak maintaining but not increasing temperature is useful, followed by switch off. As with biscuit firing, glaze firings in a 3–6 cu ft kiln may take 10–12 hours. Leave the kiln to cool to 100°C–150°C

(212°F–303°F) before pening the door. Too rapid cooling can cause dunting, where pots split apart, though this can also be induced by poor body-glaze match.

# REDUCTION

Reduction is usually associated with high-fired stonewares and porcelains of the Far East, made popular as a technique for studio potters in Britain by Bernard Leach. It is achieved by limiting the amount of air available in the firing chamber at the point when the body and glaze start to become receptive to the effects of atmosphere. Different potters have their favourite firing schedules, but most begin reduction between 900°C–1000°C (1652°F–1832°F) continuing until the end of the firing, often alternating periods of reduction with ordinary atmosphere to ensure a steady rise in temperature. Finally the reduction is cleared with a clear flame known as *the purge* which removes all soot and carbon deposits and is thought to brighten body and glaze. Some glazes require a powerful reduction until top temperature is reached.

Reduction is usually achieved in gas and oil kilns by partially closing the damper at the base of the chimney and shutting secondary inlets. This limits the input of air causing a build up of pressure in the firing chamber resulting in a smoky atmosphere and a yellow flame licking round the spy hole. Maintaining sufficient reduction and juggling with temperature rise adds to the excitement of the process. Wood fired kilns operate in a similar way with damper control, though the type of wood used can also affect the atmosphere.

# RAKU

Raku offers the opportunity to fire glazes quickly achieving spectacular effects not obtainable by other means. The process involves placing biscuited ware made from a suitable clay covered with a raku glaze in a glowing red hot kiln and rapidly bringing it to a temperature of around 900°C–1000°C (1652°F–1832°F). When the glaze has melted and matured the glowing piece is removed with tongs and either rapidly cooled in the open air and then in water, or more usually 'reduced' by plunging it in a suitable container such as a metal bin containing combustible material such as sawdust, leaves, wood chippings, and covering with a well fitting lid. The dense smoke given off blackens the body while glazes containing tin form a dark crackle, and those with copper developing attractive lustrous reds. When cool any charcoal sticking to the surface of the pot can be scrubbed away.

Raku offers unique decorative effects which, unlike traditional glaze firings, can be produced at great speed. The process is described more fully in the books listed on page 94.

57  **Gutte Eriksen** – *lotus bowl, thrown and turned, stoneware with white glaze, 11.7 cm (4¼ in.) tall, 1986. The dark body of this deceptively simple form breaking through the white opaque glaze brings out the qualities of this pot in an intriguing way*

58 *(Right)*  **David Roberts** – *bottle, coiled and thrown, with an opaque white crackle glaze, about 30 cm (12 in.) tall, c 1987. The large-scale crackle is in keeping with the monumental feel of the form*

59 *(Far right)*  **Elizabeth Raeburn** – *stemmed bowl, raku, thrown, turned and carved, about 15 cm (6 in.) tall, c 1988. The white glaze has been carefully smoked in the post-firing raku process to successfully combine form and surface texture*

# CHAPTER SEVEN

# DISCOVERING GLAZE

Most potters want to explore the range and variety of different glazes to discover for themselves what they look like and how they behave. This chapter gives recipes for a range of glazes, but as this text makes clear, simply making up a glaze from a recipe is only the start of a process of discovering the delights of glazing. The full potential of any mixture is found only by using it and discovering its qualities. Potters usually work with a small number of glazes with one or two favourites among them. A transparent, a satin matt plus one or two 'special effect' glazes are a typical repertoire. From these others can be devised. Experiments using a transparent and a semi-transparent as bases for colour and oxide additions can be instructive in discovering how they behave as well as developing new glazes, though the fluxes present will affect this.

When changing and adapting glaze add or alter only one ingredient at a time so effects can be monitored without confusion. Also keep a record of changes made so that they can be repeated. A useful start is to experiment with a transparent glaze, making it opaque by adding tin oxide or zirconium silicate, matting it or colouring it with metal oxides added either singly or in combination.

Subsequently different but similar materials in the recipe can produce subtle but significant differences. A recipe calling for feldspar, without saying which sort, refers to potash feldspar – the commonest type – but this could be replaced with soda feldspar, Cornish stone, petalite or nepheline syenite to give related but different results. Whiting can replace dolomite (and vice versa), while China clay can be replaced with ball clay, and so on. Each test will help build up knowledge of how materials behave in glazes. Observation of changes can be followed up by relating them to the chemical make-up of the materials and calculating the formula of the glaze.

## GLAZE RECIPES

The following glazes and recipes are not intended to be exhaustive, but to indicate the range and diversity of finishes available to studio potters. No matter how successful recipes may be for one potter, others may not either like the effect they obtain or be disappointed that it does not match the given description. The fired glaze depends on the clay body on which it is used, the source of the materials (many of which vary from batch to batch let alone supplier to supplier), the thickness of application, and on the speed and length of the firing. Recipes are best seen as intelligent, informed starting points rather than complete answers; some will work well the first time, other may need subtle adjustment, but with known ingredients informed changes can be made.

## RAKU

As described in Chapter 6, raku is as much a process as a description of the sort of effects that can be obtained. Glazes are made up largely of a flux such as lead, borax or alkalies used in the form of frits, together with a small amount of China clay to stabilize the mixture and help bind it on the pot. Tin oxide and zirconium silicate will opacify the glaze while metal oxides will produce a range of colours. Raku is decorative rather than functional and the fired ware will rarely be waterproof nor will the glazes be particularly safe for food. The effects obtained from raku are perhaps more variable than any other ceramics technique, depending on the thickness of application and the results of post-firing techniques of smoking. But the speed of the process and the dramatic effects make it an exciting and spectacular process.

## CLEAR RAKU GLAZES
### 900°C–1000°C (1652°F–1832°F)

| | | |
|---|---|---:|
| 1 | Lead bisilicate | 85 |
| | Flint | 5 |
| | China clay | 8 |
| | Bentonite | 2 |
| 2 | Borax frit | 90 |
| | China clay | 8 |
| | Bentonite | 2 |
| 3 | Borax frit | 70 |
| | Lead bisilicate | 20 |
| | China clay | 8 |
| | Bentonite | 2 |

Add opacifiers and colouring oxides to any of the glazes as required.

# EARTHENWARE GLAZES

**Transparent** Most potters want a good clear or transparent glaze; its smooth, even surface makes it ideal for functional ware but while its practical qualities may be highly valued, it may lack sufficient visual interest to be of general interest on its own and may benefit from small additions of an opacifier or a colouring oxide used in conjunction with decorative slips.

Most earthenware transparent glazes, such as raku, make use of commercial frits to act as fluxes to which are added some form of clay and often small quantities of feldspar and flint. Glazes fluxed by lead give the smoothest richest gloss and are generally preferred as they have a relatively wide firing range and smooth out to give an even coating. Their major disadvantage is that if poorly formulated or used in conjunction with copper the lead may be soluble if it comes into contact with weak acid solutions such as those found in food. The recipes given here are safe for functional and non-functional ware, but if modified with copper avoid using them on surfaces which come into contact with food.

## CLEAR LEAD GLAZE
### 1050°C–1100°C (1922°F–2012°F)

| | |
|---|---:|
| Lead bisilicate | 83 |
| Cornish stone | 14 |
| Bentonite | 3 |

A useful, well-fitting clear glaze.

## CLEAR LEAD/BORAX GLAZE
### 1050°C–1100°C (1922°F–2012°F)

| | |
|---|---:|
| Lead bisilicate | 58 |
| Standard borax frit | 30 |
| Feldspar | 3 |
| China clay | 9 |

A clear glaze.

## WHITE OPAQUE GLAZE
### 1050°C–1100°C (1922°F–2012°F)

| | |
|---|---:|
| Lead bisilicate | 80 |
| Feldspar | 5 |
| China clay | 15 |
| + Tin oxide | 11 |

An attractive smooth white.

**Matt** Matt glazes have a fine crystalline structure which gives them their matt, satin-like appearance. When properly compounded they are fully matured glazes with smooth surfaces.

## TITANIUM MATT GLAZE
### 1100°C (2012°F)

| | |
|---|---:|
| Lead bisilicate | 54 |
| Zinc oxide | 15 |
| Whiting | 10 |
| Feldspar | 10 |
| Flint | 5 |
| China clay | 6 |
| + Titanium dioxide | 11 |

A smooth silky matt.

## LIME MATT GLAZE
### 1050°C–1080°C (1922°F–1976°F)

| | |
|---|---|
| Lead bisilicate | 62 |
| Zinc oxide | 19 |
| Whiting | 6 |
| China clay | 22 |

A dryish matt glaze.

## ALUMINA MATT GLAZE
### 1100°C (2012°F)

| | |
|---|---|
| Lead bisilicate | 50 |
| Whiting | 10 |
| Feldspar | 20 |
| China clay | 20 |

A hard matt glaze.

**Coloured glazes** Any of the glazes listed above can be coloured or stained with metal oxides, the results influenced by the predominant flux and amount of alumina or lime present. Refer to the different oxides listed on pages 32–42 for colour possibilities. Two recipes below are particularly attractive at earthenware temperature.

## ROCKINGHAM BROWN
### 1100°C (2012°F)

| | |
|---|---|
| Lead bisilicate | 47 |
| Feldspar | 25 |
| Whiting | 5 |
| Flint | 5 |
| China clay | 18 |
| +Red iron oxide | 4 |
| Manganese dioxide | 8 |

A rich lustrous black-brown.

## AVENTURINE GLAZE
### 1070°C (1958°F)

| | |
|---|---|
| Borax frit | 35 |
| Lead bisilicate | 40 |
| Cornish stone | 20 |
| China clay | 5 |
| +Red iron oxide | 9 |
| Copper oxide | 1 |

A deep brown glaze with gold spangles.

# MEDIUM TEMPERATURE STONEWARE GLAZES 1180°C–1240°C (2155°F–2265°F)

In this range both earthenware and stoneware fluxes can be used. Lead, which starts to become volatile around 1150°C (2100°F), can continue to be active in glazes at 1220°C (2230°F), but as a general rule it ceases to be of great value at 1200°C (2192°F). Smooth transparent glazes rely on other fluxes such as calcium borate frit (or colemanite or gerstley borate) to give well melted even glazes with a wide firing range.

**Transparent** A well melted fluxed glaze is an excellent starting point from which to develop a wide range of colour and texture.

## CLEAR, TRANSPARENT GLAZE
### 1200°C–1220°C (2192°F–2228°F)

| | |
|---|---|
| Feldspar | 40 |
| Calcium borate frit (colemanite) | 35 |
| China clay | 15 |
| Flint | 10 |

A smooth well-fitting glaze.

## TRANSPARENT GLAZE
### 1200°C–1220°C (2192°F–2228°F)

| | |
|---|---|
| Nepheline syenite | 40 |
| Whiting | 15 |
| Zinc oxide | 10 |
| China clay | 5 |
| Flint | 30 |

A clear transparent glaze.

**Matt and satin matt** Matt glazes can bring out form while satin glazes have the functional qualities of glossy glazes without the reflective surface.

## SMOOTH WHITE GLAZE
### 1200°C–1220°C (2192°F–2228°F)

| | |
|---|---|
| Feldspar | 38 |
| Whiting | 12 |
| Zinc oxide | 18 |
| China clay | 27 |
| Flint | 7 |

An opaque glaze.

**Coloured glazes** For the brightest results coloured glazes depend on the body of the pot. Dark bodies can break through edges and rims of opaque and matt glazes to good effect, but bright colours require a light coloured body with a low iron content as the interaction between clay and glaze is greatly increased at this temperature. While coloured glazes can be opacified this can have a muting effect on the colour. Small amounts of lithium, a flux active over a wide range of temperature, will enliven glaze and encourage a brighter response from metal oxides particularly from copper, manganese and chrome which will yield respectively turquoise blue, mauve purple and yellow green.

## MATT ALKALINE BASE GLAZE
### 1200°C–1260°C (2192°F–2300°F)

| | |
|---|---|
| Nepheline syenite | 55 |
| Barium carbonate | 25 |
| Lithium carbonate | 2 |
| Flint | 8 |
| China clay | 6 |

A smooth satin glaze. With copper carbonate 3% a bright turquoise results. This glaze responds well with additions of other oxides.

# STONEWARE GLAZES
# 1240°C–1280°C
# (2264°F–2336°F)

Many of the glazes listed in the previous section can be adjusted to fire to higher temperatures by lowering the fluxes and increasing the clay and flint. The range of colours and textures available at stoneware temperatures are extensive; effects are determined by the fluxes present in the glaze, by the atmosphere of the firing and by the body of the pot. From one or two basic glazes a variety of results can be evolved and this method is recommended for potters wanting to develop a personal repertoire of glazes. Major fluxes for higher temperature glazes are calcium (present in wollastonite, whiting and dolomite), magnesium (present in dolomite and talc), zinc oxide, potassium and sodium (present in feldspars).

**Transparent glazes** Some of the simplest and cheapest transparent glazes are combinations of feldspar, whiting and clay. By juggling with the proportions glazes can be made harder or softer, clear, matt or satin. As a general guide Bernard Leach's classic transparent recipe for a feldspathic transparent glaze is a good starting point.

## LEACH TRANSPARENT CONE 8 GLAZE
### 1260°C (2300°F)

| | |
|---|---|
| Feldspar | 40 |
| Flint | 30 |
| Whiting | 20 |
| China clay | 10 |

This glaze can be adapted to make it slightly more fusible:

| | |
|---|---|
| Feldspar | 50 |
| Flint | 15 |
| Whiting | 15 |
| China clay | 20 |

A further variation which will fire to a higher temperature is:

| | |
|---|---|
| Feldspar | 30 |
| Whiting | 25 |
| Flint | 20 |
| China clay | 25 |

Another classic clear feldspathic glaze is:

| | |
|---|---|
| Feldspar | 78 |
| Whiting | 19 |
| Bentonite | 3 |

The atmosphere of the kiln will affect the degree of melt of all of these feldspathic glazes.

**Matt and satin glazes** The commonest and most popular smooth matt glazes, both in electric kilns and reduction firings, are ones containing magnesium. At their best such glazes tend to be creamy white, opaque and smooth. Other matt glazes include high alumina glazes which tend to be less smooth and often have a drier surface, more suitable for decorative rather than functional pots. Matt glazes rich in zinc or barium will yield special colour responses.

## DOLOMITE MATT GLAZE
### 1260°C (2300°F)

| | |
|---|---|
| Feldspar | 10 |
| Nepheline syenite | 24 |
| Dolomite | 19 |
| Whiting | 5 |
| China clay | 20 |
| Flint | 20 |

A smooth dry matt. The following is a more satin dolomite:

| | |
|---|---|
| Potash feldspar | 10 |
| Soda feldspar | 30 |
| Whiting | 15 |
| Dolomite | 20 |
| Flint | 5 |
| China clay | 20 |

**Zinc glazes** At stoneware temperatures, zinc oxide will act as a flux though if present in large amounts will tend to make glazes opaque.

## A SMOOTH CLEAR GLAZE
### 1260°C (2300°F)

| | |
|---|---|
| Feldspar | 44 |
| Whiting | 15 |
| Talc | 8 |
| Zinc oxide | 8 |
| Flint | 20 |
| China clay | 5 |

An attractive clear glaze in electric kilns and in reduction. It is also a sound base for the addition of metal oxides.

**Iron glazes** At stoneware temperature iron is extremely versatile giving a wide range of colours depending on the amount of iron and the fluxes present and the firing atmosphere. Calcium is the flux most favoured to bring out the full qualities of the oxide; it encourages bright colours and by readily allowing iron to go into solution delicate shades can be obtained as well as stronger dark browns and blacks. In small amounts (1%) iron will give blues in reduction in glazes free of titania which turns the iron green – known as *celadons*. Some 8–12% is required to produce rich black tenmokus which break a bright rust orange on rims and edges. The best tenmokus need a temperature of around 1270°C–1280°C (2318°F–2336°F) to develop depth of colour. In glazes containing 8–10% bone ash, similar amounts of iron will yield rich orange-red colours often with darker mottled shading. Amounts of iron greater than 12% tend to saturate the glaze which, during the cooling, crystallize out to give what is called tea-dust or khaki effects – an opaque reddish-brown matrix with small rust red crystals. Oil spot glazes often made up of large quantities of iron-bearing earths such as yellow ochre, form decorative spots of lustrous silver in a dark brown or black background. While highly attractive, such effects can be elusive.

## CELADON

| | |
|---|---|
| Feldspar | 40 |
| Whiting | 15 |
| Ball clay | 6 |
| China clay | 4 |
| Flint | 35 |
| + Red iron oxide | 2% |

A rich celadon green in reduction, a muted pale olive in the electric kiln.

## TENMOKU

| | |
|---|---|
| Feldspar | 35 |
| Whiting | 18 |
| Flint | 37 |
| China clay | 10 |
| + Red iron oxide | 11% |

## RICH IRON-ORANGE RED

| | |
|---|---|
| Feldspar | 56 |
| Talc | 9 |
| Bone ash | 9 |
| China clay | 10 |
| Flint | 16 |
| + Red iron oxide | 8% |

**Shino** Our appreciation of many of the qualities of high-fired glazes comes from the great ceramic tradition of Japan, in particular on vessels used in the tea ceremony where the qualities of different glazes are carefully studied and appreciated. Shino glazes, characterized by a grey-white background breaking a rich orange and gold, were fired slowly in long climbing kilns to allow the full effects of the interaction of body, glaze and heat to be fully developed. The subtle but rich shino effect is almost impossible to obtain in electric kilns, requiring the smoky atmosphere of reduction to realize the effect. Shino glazes are relatively simple to make up and require alkaline flux and a small amount of iron.

## SHINO

| | |
|---|---|
| Nepheline syenite | 30 |
| Feldspar | 30 |
| Petalite | 6 |
| Ball clay | 34 |

(the ball clay needs to contain about 3–4% iron oxide)

**Copper reds** In reduction atmospheres in suitable glaze formations copper changes from its usual green to its more unusual red state. The brightest reds, known as *flambé* and *sang-de-boeuf*, are achieved by very small amounts of copper, usually of about 0.5%. A small quantity of tin oxide helps to stabilize the colour. Glazes which fire turquoise in electric kilns often yield a range of reds in reduction firings.

60   **Ursula Schied** – *porcelain bowl, thrown and turned with carved decoration, 12 cm (5 in.) tall, 1984. The matt glaze has been flashed pink by copper in the kiln adding to the fragility and delicacy of this bowl*

## COPPER RED (REDUCTION)

| | |
|---|---|
| Feldspar | 57 |
| Barium carbonate | 18 |
| Dolomite | 5 |
| Flint | 10 |
| China clay | 5 |
| + Copper carbonate | 1.5% |
| Tin oxide | 2.5% |

A strong reduction is required.

In electric kilns reduction can be achieved in the glaze by the addition of small amounts of silicon carbide. A powerful flux such as calcium borate frit or borax frit is needed to break down the silicon carbide while the glaze also needs to be sufficiently fluid to allow the gas formed to be released if a smooth surface is required.

## RICH, DEEP RED

| | |
|---|---|
| Soda feldspar | 52 |
| Calcium borate frit (or gerstley borate) | 10 |
| Whiting | 15 |
| China clay | 5 |
| Flint | 18 |
| + Copper carbonate | 0.5% |
| Tin oxide | 1% |
| Silicon carbide (fine) | 0.5% |

## MUTED PINK GREY

| | |
|---|---|
| Feldspar | 37 |
| Calcium borate frit (or gerstley borate) | 6 |
| Whiting | 20 |
| Talc | 5 |
| Flint | 30 |
| China clay | 5 |
| + Silicon carbide | 0.5% |
| Copper carbonate | 1% |

**Crystalline glazes** Matt glazes, created by a matrix of fine crystals formed within the glaze, can, under certain circumstances, be made to form large sized individual crystals. In crystalline glazes the ingredients go into a saturated solution at top temperature and as they slowly cool crystals form in the matrix of the glaze. The problem is to achieve a balance between making the glaze sufficiently molten so that a complete degree of melt is achieved while it is not so fluid that the glaze runs off the pot. During cooling the temperature needs to be held to allow crystals to form. Crystalline glazes are low in alumina to encourage crystal growth – a further difficulty in achieving successful, stable glazes. Crystalline glazes can be stained with small amounts of metal oxides and crystals will be selective in taking up different colours. Some glazes will develop attractive crystals without holding the temperature while cooling though these will be small in comparison with those which can be encouraged to grow by maintaining a

temperature plateau. For stoneware glazes the plateau is around 1100°C (2012°F); for earthenware 800°C (1472°F).

61 (*Right*)  **Eileen Lewenstein** – Dark Spring and High Summer, *two porcelain vases, thrown and turned, fired to 1250°C (2282°F) in electric kiln, tallest 25 cm (10 in.), 1990. The matt glaze (feldspar 4, whiting 32, China clay 40, flint 18, dolomite 7) has colouring oxides added to achieve the staining effects. The pale yellow glaze has 0.5 to 0.75% iron oxide, the dark green has small additions of copper and iron oxide (Collection North Central Washington Museum, Wenatchee, WA, USA)*

62 (*Far right*)  **Derek Clarkson** – *porcelain bottle, thrown and turned with crystalline glaze, electric kiln, 12 cm (5 in.) tall, 1991. The green crystals on this bottle are visually effective and well suited to the form.* RECIPE: *ferro frit 3110 42, calcined zinc oxide 31.5, flint 20, titanium dioxide 5.5, alumina hydrate 0.4, China clay 0.6 + copper carbonate 6; the glaze is fired to 1260°C (2300°F) then cooled to 1095°C (2000°F) and the temperature held for 1 hour 25 minutes, then cooled to 1065°C (1949°F) and held for 1 hour 30 minutes then cooled to 1055°C (1931°F) and held for 15 minutes, cooled to 1045°C (1920°F) and held for 15 minutes before allowing it to cool completely*

## ZINC SILICATE CRYSTALLINE GLAZE 1
### Electric kiln 1260°C (2300°F)

| | |
|---|---|
| High alkaline frit | 44 |
| Feldspar | 7 |
| Zinc oxide | 36 |
| Whiting | 3 |
| Flint | 7 |
| China clay | 3 |
| + Rutile | 3% |
| Nickel oxide | 1% |

Other oxides will produce different colours.

## ZINC SILICATE CRYSTALLINE GLAZE 2

| | |
|---|---|
| Feldspar | 35 |
| Zinc oxide | 25 |
| Whiting | 14 |
| Flint | 21 |
| China clay | 5 |
| + Rutile | 4% |

**Turquoise** In high alkaline glazes copper will yield bright turquoise, rather than the more usual green, in silky matt or dry surfaced glazes. A typical recipe includes nepheline syenite, barium carbonate and/or lithium carbonate plus 2–3% copper oxide. Many glazes work only in electric kilns, others are effective in all atmospheres. Because of the high barium content such glazes are not recommended for use on functional wares.

## BARIUM MATT SMOOTH TURQUOISE SEA GREEEN

| | |
|---|---|
| Feldspar | 55 |
| Dolomite | 5 |
| Barium carbonate | 20 |
| Flint | 10 |
| China clay | 10 |
| + Copper carbonate | 2% |

This fires a deep red in reduction. If nepheline syenite is substituted for the feldspar a drier, more matt turquoise results.

## A SMOOTH RICH TURQUOISE

| | |
|---|---|
| Nephiline syenite | 55 |
| Barium carbonate | 25 |
| Lithium carbonate | 2 |
| Flint | 8 |
| China clay | 6 |
| + Copper oxide | 3% |

This glaze has a wide firing temperature.

**Pink and red glazes** Apart from reduction fired copper, pink and red glazes can be obtained from small quantities of chrome and tin oxide, and from nickel oxide in glazes containing barium carbonate and zinc oxide. Altering the ratio of barium to zinc changes the colour response of the nickel from pink to blue. Small additions of cobalt with nickel will result in purples.

## CHROME PINK 1

| | |
|---|---|
| Cornish stone (or Cornwall stone) | 50 |
| Whiting | 30 |
| Flint | 5 |
| China clay | 15 |
| + Tin oxide | 5% |
| Chrome oxide | 0.2% |

A smooth bright pink. A larger amount of chrome will darken the red to a crimson.

## CHROME PINK 2

| | |
|---|---|
| Soda feldspar | 62 |
| Whiting | 28 |
| China clay | 10 |
| + Tin oxide | 6% |
| Chrome oxide | 0.5% |

A dryish matt pink.

## NICKEL PINK

| | |
|---|---|
| Feldspar | 33 |
| Barium carbonate | 39 |
| Zinc oxide | 16 |
| China clay | 5 |
| Flint | 6 |
| + Nickel oxide | 1.5% |

A bright nickel pink, more blue when thin.

**Ash glazes** Wood ash is one of the oldest glaze materials for high temperature glazes. It has little or no value at earthenware temperatures. Variable from batch to batch and from ash to ash it has to be tested each time the supply changes, but can produce attractive mottled effects. Wood ash is a complex material, high in fluxes and silica – almost a glaze in itself. Used alone, mixed wood ash or that from hard woods will form a thin pigment-like layer on the surface of the clay at stoneware temperature. Simple combinations of wood ash and ball clay, or wood ash and feldspar are particularly effective at bringing out the characteristic qualities of wood ash. Alternatives to wood ash which behave in a similar way can be made up from a judicious mixture of local clays and fluxes. Sometimes known as synthetic wood ash, they are reliable and often more dramatic in their effect than wood ash. As such mixtures need to be highly fluxed to break and be fluid at top temperature, they pose problems in preventing them running off the pot.

*63* **Emmanuel Cooper** - *stoneware bowl, thrown and turned with glaze made only out of mixed wood ash, 15 cm (6 in.) diameter, electric kiln, 1980. The characteristic runs of the ash glaze fit the simple direct bowl form*

## SYNTHETIC ASH GLAZE

| | |
|---|---|
| Cornish stone | 35 |
| Whiting | 45 |
| Dolomite | 5 |
| China clay | 15 |
| + Iron oxide | 2% |

A runny, mottled surface; do not apply too thickly.

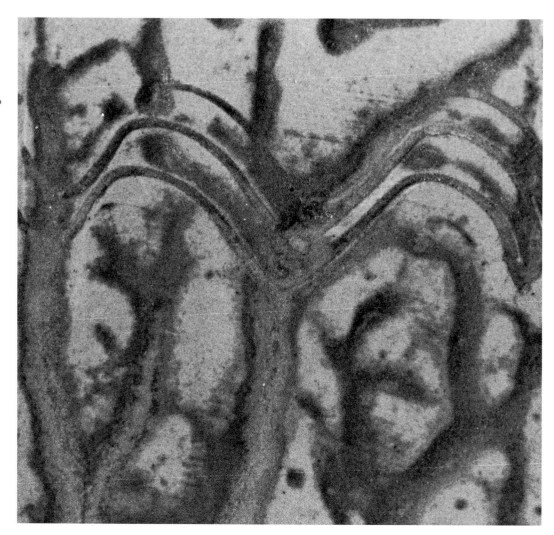

64   *A simulated ash-type stoneware glaze, applied over a buff firing stoneware body, which needs careful application and firing to prevent undue running.* RECIPE: *feldspar 12, whiting 60, China clay 20, flint 4, talc 10, bone ash 6*

# APPENDIX

## COMMON CERAMIC MATERIALS

| | Chemical symbol | Molecular weight |
|---|---|---|
| Alumina hydrate | $Al(OH)_3$ | Eq wt 78 |
| Barium carbonate (witherite) | $BaCO_3$ | 197.4 |
| Bone ash (calcium phosphate) | $3CaO.P_2O_5$ or | 310.2 |
| | $Ca_3(PO_4)_2$ | Eq wt 103 |
| Borax | $Na_2O.2B_2O_3.10H_2O$ | 381.5 |
| Boric acid | $B_2O_3.3H_2O$ | 123.7 |
| Boric oxide | $B_2O_3$ | 70 |
| Boro-calcite | $CaO.2B_2O_3.6H_2O$ | 304 |
| Calcium carbonate (whiting) | $CaCO_3$ | 100.1 |
| China clay | $Al_2O_3.2SiO_2.2H_2O$ | 258.1 |
| Chrome oxide | $Cr_2O_3$ | 152 |
| Cobalt oxide | $CoO$ | 74.9 |
| Colemanite | $2CaO.3B_2O_3.5H_2O$ | 412 Eq wt 206 |
| Cornish stone (Cornwall stone) | $K_2O.Al_2O_3.8SiO_2$ | 678 |
| Copper carbonate | $CuCO_3$ | 221.2 |
| Copper oxide | $CuO$ | 79.6 |
| Dolomite | $CaCO_3.MgCO_3(CaO.MgO.2CO_2)$ | 184 |
| Feldspar (potash) | $K_2O.Al_2O_3.6SiO_2$ | 556.5 |
| Feldspar (soda) | $Na_2O.Al_2O_3.6SiO_2$ | 524.3 |
| Ferric (iron) oxide | $Fe_2O_3$ | 159.7 |
| Flint (quartz) | $SiO_2$ | 60.1 |
| Ilmenite | $FeO.TiO_2$ | 152 |

| | Chemical symbol | Molecular weight |
|---|---|---|
| Lead bisilicate | $PbO.2SiO_2$ | 343.3 |
| Lead monosilicate | $PbO.SiO_2$ | 283.3 |
| Lead oxide (litharge) | $PbO$ | 223.2 |
| Lead sesquisilicate | $2PbO.3SiO_2$ | 646.9 Eq wt 323.4 |
| Lithium oxide (lithia) | $Li_2O$ | 29.9 |
| Magnesium oxide (magnesia) | $MgO$ | 40.3 |
| Manganese carbonate | $MnCO_3$ | 115 |
| Manganese dioxide | $MnO_2$ | 87 |
| Nepheline syenite | $K_2O.3Na_2O.4Al_2O_3.8SiO_2$ | 1168 Eq wt 389 |
| Nickel oxide | $NiO$ | 75 |
| Petalite | $Li_2O.Al_2O_3.8SiO_2$ | 612 |
| Silicon carbide (carborundum) | $SiC$ | 40.3 |
| Talc (steatite, french chalk) | $3MgO.4SiO_2.H_2O$ | 380 Eq wt 127 |
| Tin oxide (stannic oxide) | $SnO_2$ | 151 |
| Titanium oxide (anatase) | $TiO_2$ | 80 |
| Vanadium pentoxide | $V_2O_5$ | 182 |
| Wollastonite | $CaSiO_3$ | 116 |
| Zinc oxide | $ZnO$ | 81 |
| Zirconium oxide (zirconia) | $ZrO_2$ | 123 |

*Equivalent weights*
Some materials have 'equivalent weights'. This defines the molecular weight of the material which must be taken to yield one complete unit of the oxide desired in the glaze. Most materials have the same molecular and equivalent weights.

# GLAZE CALCULATIONS

## GLAZE RECIPE TO GLAZE FORMULA USING THE SIMPLIFIED METHOD

Once the basic steps for calculating the composition of a glaze have been understood, then the method can be applied to any recipe. See page 87 and left for molecular weights (MW).

### EXAMPLE 1

To calculate the formula for a stoneware glaze recipe firing to 1260°C (2300°F) feldspar 70, whiting 20, China clay 10:

| Recipe | | Formula | Molecular weight |
|---|---|---|---|
| Feldspar | 70 | $K_2O.Al_2O_3.6SiO_2$ | 556 |
| Whiting | 20 | $CaCO_3$ | 100 |
| China clay | 10 | $Al_2O_3.2SiO_2.2H_2O$ | 258 |

**1** First find the proportion of the molecules of each ingredient present in the glaze and divide each quantity by its molecular weight:

$$\frac{\text{parts by weight}}{\text{molecular weight}} = \text{molecular parts}$$

Feldspar $\dfrac{70}{556} = 0.126$ molecular parts

Whiting $\dfrac{20}{100} = 0.200$ molecular parts

China clay $\dfrac{10}{258} = 0.039$ molecular parts

**2** Find the proportion of each oxide in each material by multiplying the molecular parts by the number of molecules present in the formula:

|  | $K_2O$ | $Al_2O_3$ | $SiO_2$ |  | CaO |
|---|---|---|---|---|---|
| Feldspar | 0.126 | 0.126 | 0.756 | $(0.126 \times 6)$ | — |
| Whiting | — | — | — |  | 0.20 |
| China clay | — | 0.039 | 0.078 | $(0.039 \times 2)$ | — |
| Totals | 0.126 | 0.165 | 0.834 |  | 0.20 |

This may now be written as the formula:

$K_2O$ 0.126   $Al_2O_3$ 0.165   $SiO_2$ 0.834
CaO   0.200
_____
0.326

This formula can be more easily compared with others if the total of all the fluxes adds up to 1, or unity. This is simply achieved by dividing the figures of all the ingredients in the formula by the total of the fluxes (ie 0.326). The formula now reads:

$K_2O$ 0.387   $Al_2O_3$ 0.506   $SiO_2$ 2.558
CaO   0.613

The interpretation of the formula to indicate the sort of glaze it will give depends on comparing it with the established limits for particular glazes. Calculating formulae from practical glazes can provide a store of interpretative information which can form the basis of comparison. One key is the proportion between the alumina and silica

which determines whether the glaze will be matt or shiny. The general guide for transparent glazes is the ratio 1:10, and for a matt glaze 1:5. In the above example the ratio is roughly 1:5 which suggests a matt glaze. The high proportion of calcium indicates it will encourage good responses to iron. The example of calculating the recipe given above is the simplified method which treats each material present in the glaze as a single material with its own molecular weight. This does not take into account the variability of materials, each of which has a specific analysis; this can usually be obtained from suppliers enabling more detailed calculations to be made.

Calculations are made easier if the steps are laid out on a chart such as the one illustrated overleaf (page 90).

EXAMPLE 2

## GLAZE FORMULA TO GLAZE RECIPE

Working from formula to recipe enables glazes to be calculated according to theoretical guidelines, with fluxes selected for the qualities they give to the glaze. Again, a chart such as the one illustrated on page 91, showing the different steps, makes this process much simpler.

The following stoneware glaze has a shiny finish:

CaO   0.80   $Al_2O_3$   0.60   $SiO_2$   3.0
$K_2O$   0.10
ZnO   0.10

To translate the formula to a recipe:

**1** Choose materials which will give the required oxides; the obvious choices are whiting, feldspar, zinc oxide, China clay and flint.

**2** Draw up a table showing the raw materials and the quantity of each oxide required.

*Raw material*     CaO   $K_2O$   ZnO   $Al_2O_3$   $SiO_2$
*Amount required* 0.80   0.10   0.10   0.60   3.0

**3** Fill in the chart, one material at a time. First whiting ($CaCO_3$). CaO 0.80 is called for and as whiting contains only calcium, the ratio of whiting required is 1 (the number of molecules of CaO in whiting) $\times 0.80 = 0.80$. Write this under the CaO column with a line drawn underneath to indicate this requirement is satisfied. Repeat this procedure for ZnO for which 0.10 is required. As zinc oxide (ZnO) contains only zinc the amount required is calculated by multiplying the amount called for (0.10) with the number of molecules of zinc in zinc oxide (1) $= 0.10$. This figure is written under the ZnO column.

**4** The next material, feldspar, is more complex as it contains three materials present

RECIPE TO FORMULA: QUICK METHOD

| Description of glaze | | | | Oxides Present in glaze materials | | | | | | | | | | | | | | | | | | | |
|---|---|---|---|---|---|---|---|---|---|---|---|---|---|---|---|---|---|---|---|---|---|---|---|
| Materials & Formula | Quantity in recipe | Molecular weight | = Molecular Proportion | | | | | | | | | | | | | | | | | | | | |
| | | | | | | | | | | | | | | | | | | | | | | | |
| | | TOTALS: | | | | | | | | | | | | | | | | | | | | | |

Reduce formula to unify by dividing all totals by total of bases.

3    Formula with one decimal point.

FORMULA TO RECIPE: QUICK METHOD

Glaze Formula

Firing temperature

Glaze description

| Oxides required | | | | | | | | | | | Ratio | × | Mol. | | % | |
|---|---|---|---|---|---|---|---|---|---|---|---|---|---|---|---|---|
| Amount needed | | | | | | | | | | | | | Weight | | | |
| Source | | | | | | | | | | | | | | | | |

in different proportions. Each molecule of feldspar contains one of $K_2O$, therefore the ratio of feldspar required to satisfy this is $1 \times 0.10 = 0.10$ which is put in the $K_2O$ column and a line drawn. As feldspar also contains one molecule of $Al_2O_3$ the same amount (0.10) is entered in the $Al_2O_3$ column, and subtracted from the total of $Al_2O_3$ required (0.60) leaving 0.50 still to be found. In addition feldspar also contains 6 molecules of silica ($SiO_2$) and therefore the ratio supplied by 0.10 is $0.10 \times 6 = 0.60$. This sum is entered in the $SiO_2$ column and subtracted from the total required.

The amounts still to be satisfied are 0.50 $Al_2O_3$ and 2.40 $SiO_2$ which can be satisfied with China clay and flint using the same method. For the alumina in the China clay 0.50 is needed which goes in the $Al_2O_3$ column; for the silica the amount of 0.50 is multiplied by 2 as China clay contains 2 molecules of $SiO_2$ giving 1 part of $SiO_2$

($2 \times 0.50$) which is entered in the $SiO_2$ column and subtracted from the amount needed leaving 1.40 still required. This is satisfied by entering 1.40 parts of flint so completing the chart (see below).

5 The ratio of the molecules of the raw materials have now been found and have to be converted into the physical weight of each material. This is done by multiplying each ratio by its molecular weight:

Whiting $0.80 \times 100 = 80$
Zinc oxide $0.10 \times 81 = 8.10$
Feldspar $0.10 \times 556 = 55.60$
China clay $0.50 \times 258 = 129$
Flint $1.40 \times 60 = 84$

Total $\underline{356.7}$

6 The recipe is converted into percentage figures by dividing each amount by the sum

of all the ingredients (356.7) and multiplying by 100 to give the following recipe in round numbers:

Whiting 22
Zinc oxide 2
Feldspar 16
China clay 37
Flint 23

## UK/USA EQUIVALENT MATERIALS

Materials available in one country are not necessarily the same as those in another despite the fact that they have the same chemical formulae. Minerals used by potters rarely have precise composition and vary from batch to batch, let alone country to country. However, many straightforward substitutions can be made.

**Bone ash** In glazes natural or synthetic bone ash can be used.

**Local clays** Glazes which call for local clay usually refer to a fine particle sized clay which contains some 4%–6% iron and are fusible at relatively low temperatures and so in high temperature glazes can serve as fluxes as well as sources of alumina. With such a general material testing available clays is essential and can result in interesting glazes.

**Ball clays** are usually highly plastic and white firing (though may appear black in their raw state because of their carbon content which

| Raw material with formula | Ratio needed | CaO 0.80 | ZnO 0.10 | $K_2O$ 0.10 | $Al_2O_3$ 0.60 | $SiO_2$ 3.0 |
|---|---|---|---|---|---|---|
| Whiting $CaCO_3$ | 0.80 | 0.80 | — | — | — | — |
| Zinc oxide ZnO | 0.10 | — | 0.10 | — | — | — |
| Feldspar $K_2O.Al_2O_3.6SiO_2$ | 0.10 | — | — | 0.10 | 0.10 0.50 | 0.60 2.40 |
| China clay $Al_2O_3.2SiO_2.2H_2O$ | 0.50 | — | — | — | 0.50 | 1.00 1.40 |
| Flint $SiO_2$ | 1.40 | — | — | — | — | 1.40 |

burns out during the firing). They vary from mine to mine. Some are high in silica, others in alumina and no two are the same. Typical UK ball clays are TWVD, SMD Hymod, Hyplass; USA – Kentucky OM4, Kentucky Special, Tennessee No 5.

**China clay** (kaolin) Though all China clays have the same theoretical formula there are variations in particle size and plasticity. Grolleg is a high quality plastic China clay produced in the UK. EPK is a more plastic China clay from Florida. Calcined China clay, called molochite, is pre-fired and can be added to glazes to reduce their plastic content.

**Colemanite** and **gerstley borate** are sources of boron, a highly active flux. Gerstley borate is more useful as some forms of colemanite cause the glaze to spit off the surface during the early part of the firing as water is given off rapidly. A near equivalent in the UK is calcium borate frit.

**Feldspars** In the UK feldspars are described by their major flux. The most common is potash, and the one used when no specific spar is called for; it contains potassium oxide; soda feldspar contains sodium oxide. In the USA potash is known as Custer, Bell, Buckingham G200, Kingman, K 200, Clinchfield no 202, G22; soda as F-4 Kona.

**Cornish stone** (or sometimes just Stone) in the UK is known in the USA as Cornwall, Carolina stone, Kona A-4 and pyrophyllite.

**Frits** Different manufacturers produce a wide range of frits, some of which are similar to those of other makers. For direct equivalents the chemical formula will have to be consulted though this is not always disclosed. The three types of lead frit – monosilicate, sesquisilicate and bisilicate are fairly standard and can be readily substituted. Borax frits are also similar though rarely identical. High alkaline frits such as Ferro 3110 and Ferro 5301 have no direct equivalents and experiments will have to be made to achieve similar effects.

**Zirconium silicate** is an opacifier sometimes known as zircon and dispersion in the UK; in the USA it is sold under the trade names of *Opax, Superpax, Zircopax*.

# PROTECTING YOUR HEALTH

Many of the materials used for making glazes are potentially hazardous if taken into the body. A few such as wood ash may irritate the skin while others may build up slowly in the body and may pose a long term threat to health. In its dry powdered form any glaze material can be inhaled and may cause damage. Continued exposure adds to the problem. The most dangerous airborne dust is flint or quartz (silica); over time this can build up in the lungs and in extreme cases can lead to silicosis. Other materials may cause different problems, and prevention is always better than cure; use moist flint and keep dust to a minimum.

Though most precautions are commonsense, it is necessary to become health conscious and the following precautions will help:

1 Do not eat, drink or smoke in the pottery workshop.
2 Keep the workshop as dust free as possible. Avoid sweeping other than by using a suitable compound, but sponge or wet wipe to prevent rising dust.
3 Wear protective clothing such as overalls and aprons. Launder them regularly. Synthetic fabrics retain less dust than cotton or other natural fibres.
4 When mixing glazes wear protective gloves to prevent absorption through the skin.
5 Wear a recommended face mask to prevent inhaling dust.
6 When cleaning kiln shelves wear protective goggles to prevent flying chips or splinters damaging eyes.
7 Only peer into a hot kiln when wearing suitable spectacles with a blue lens or use a face shield with a blue lens window. Blue lenses cut out harmful rays while the shield prevents damaging blasts of hot air.
8 Keep the kiln room well ventilated to remove fumes given off during firing.
9 Keep all materials covered and clearly labelled so you know what you are using.
10 Be sensible about the risks involved and take no chances.

# FURTHER READING

Byers Ian *Raku* Batsford, London 1990. A beautifully illustrated practical guide to this exciting and spectacular process.

Caiger-Smith Alan *Tin-Glazed Pottery in Europe and the Islamic World* Faber and Faber, London 1973. A historical survey and a practical guide to working with reduction-fired majolica and lustre.

Clinton Margery *Lustres* Batsford, London 1992. A comprehensive introduction to creating successful lustres.

Colbeck, John *Pottery: Techniques of Decoration* Batsford 1983. A useful and practical guide.

Cooper Emmanuel and Royle Derek *Glazes for the Studio Potter* Batsford, London 1978. A comprehensive book on understanding, preparing, devising and firing as well as the chemistry of glazes.

Cooper Emmanuel *The Potter's Book of Glaze Recipes* Batsford, London 1980. Over 500 recipes covering all temperatures, annotated to indicate the results in electric and flame-burning kilns.

Cooper Emmanuel *Electric Kiln Pottery* Batsford, London 1982. A guide to making full and creative use of clay bodies and glazes in electric kilns.

Cooper Emmanuel *Cooper's Book of Glaze Recipes* Batsford, London 1987. A further selection of glaze recipes all fully annotated with firing details.

Cooper Emmanuel *A History of World Pottery* Batsford, London 1988. A general history of ceramics which illustrates the range and diversity of pots of the past.

Hamer, Frank and Janet *The Potter's Dictionary of Materials and Techniques* A & C Black, London (3rd edition) 1991. An excellent general reference book, written by potters for potters.

**Ceramic magazines**

*Ceramic Review*
21 Carnaby Street
London W1V 1PH

*Ceramics Monthly*
Box 12448
Columbus
Ohio 43212

*Ceramic Art and Perception*
35 William Street
Paddington
NSW 2021

*Pottery in Australia*
2/68 Alexander Street
Crows Nest
NSW 2065

# ADDRESSES OF SUPPLIERS

## UK

Potterycrafts Ltd
Campbell Road
Stoke-on-Trent ST4 4ET
*Raw materials, clays, colours, kilns, etc*

Potclays Ltd
Brick Kiln Lane
Etruria
Stoke-on-Trent ST4 7BP
*Raw materials, clays, oxides, colours, kilns, etc*

The Fulham Pottery Ltd
8–10 Ingate Place
Battersea
London SW8 3NS
*Clays, raw materials, oxides and kilns*

Reward Products Europe Ltd
Unit A Brookhouse Industrial Estate
Cheadle
Stoke-on-Trent ST10 1PW
*Glazes, slips, oxides, machinery*

## USA

Amaco American Art Clay Co Inc
4717 W 16th Street
Indianapolis
IN 46222
*Colours, kilns, materials*

Bailey Pottery Equipment Corp
CPO Box 1577
Kingston
New York NY 12401
*Kilns*

Mid-South Ceramic Supply Company
1230 4th Avenue
N Nashville
TN 37208
*Glazes*

Bennett's
4205 Norton Avenue
Orlando
FL 32805
*Kilns, clays, wheels, slips, glazes, tools*

Alpine
1555 Louis Avenue
Elk Grove Village
IL 60007
*Oxides, wheels, clays, kilns*

Continental Clay Company
1101 Stinson Blvd, N E
Minneapolis, Min 55413
*Clays*

## AUSTRALIA

Potters Equipment Pty Ltd
13/42 New Street
Ringwood
Victoria 3134
*Clays, glazes, kilns, materials*

Keane Ceramics Pty Ltd
Box 10202
Gosford South
NSW 2250
*Pottery materials, kilns, wheels, equipment*

Ceramic Supply Company
61 Lakemba Street
Belmore
NSW 2192
*Glazes, clays, kilns, wheels*

# INDEX